HOCKEY

DREAMS

*Memories
of a Man Who
Couldn't Play*

HOCKEY
DREAMS

*Memories
of a Man Who
Couldn't Play*

David Adams Richards

Anchor Canada

Anchor Canada and colophon are trademarks.

National Library of Canada Cataloguing in Publication Data

Richards, David Adams, 1950–
  Hockey dreams : memories of a man who couldn't play

ISBN 0-385-65856-7

1. Hockey – Canada. 2. Richards, David Adams, 1950–   . I. Title.

GV848.4.C3R53 2001   796.962'0971   C2001-930658-X

Cover image by Hulton Getty
Cover design by Linda Gustafson / Counterpunch
Text design by Heidy Lawrance Associates
Printed and bound in Canada

Visit Random House of Canada Limited's website:
www. randomhouse.ca

TRANS 10 9 8 7 6 5 4 3 2 1

To the memory of Kevin Casey,
who always knew why the
puck was dropped.

ACKNOWLEDGEMENTS

I would like to thank Mr. John Carleton, Mr. Jeffery Carleton, with a special thanks to Mr. Ron Cook.

I am also indebted to Scott Young's *War on Ice* and David Cruise and Alison Griffiths' *Net Worth*.

Part One

ONE

I WAS FIVE THOUSAND MILES away from home, in the middle of the mountains of British Columbia, in the middle of winter. On a reading tour, in 1989, I was going from town to town while the snow fell, covering up the small roads along the mountain passes.

I was billeted at different houses, and would often find myself in a strange little village, at a stranger's house at midnight. And since I'm a night person I found myself sitting in uncomfortable positions reading cookbooks at one o'clock in the morning.

One of the people who billeted me, I did become quite fond of. He was a man who had moved here with his wife from the United States a number of years before, during the "back to the land" movement. He was very kind to me, although I disagreed with him on the back to the land movement itself. And nothing he told me did anything but reinforce my bias.

But I gave him the greatest compliment I could. I told him he reminded me of my friend Stafford Foley — a boy I grew up with, way back in the Maritimes. Both of them were quite small men, with a great kind-heartedness.

I left his house on a Thursday morning to go to another village, some 40 miles away where I had a reading.

"If you ever need a place to stay again —" he said, "at any time — look me up." He handed me his telephone number.

I told him I would.

It had been snowing for four days. The snowflakes were as big as sugar cookies.

By Thursday night I found myself in an untenable position. It was one of those nights when I wanted to be anywhere but where I was. I had been with my new host fifteen minutes, and already a tense discussion had taken place.

I was honour bred. I knew I could no longer stay in his house. But where would I go? It was after ten at night. The roads were all blocked.

I telephoned my little back-to-the-land friend some 40 miles away. "You have to come and get me," I whispered.

"Now?" he said.

"If you don't mind. You wouldn't have a skidoo or something?"

"No, I have no skidoo — I'd have to take the car."

"Car is fine — I like a car —"

"But it's snowing —"

"Yes."

4

"What happened?"

"It would be better if you just came and got me as quickly as possible —" I said.

"If I go over the mountain pass — I won't be found until next spring —"

(long pause)

"I know, I know, but desperate circumstances call for desperate measures. That's a chance I'm willing that you take." I sighed.

I said my goodbye to the host, and stood outside the house with my suitcase. The man looked out the window at me now and again, as I waited for my friend, and closed the curtains when I glanced back at him.

Snowstorms were different in this part of Canada. But it was still Canada, dark and gloomy.

It had all started because of a thought I shared that evening. I had thought at supper, that from this part of the world — at this very time of year, in 1961 the Trail Smoke Eaters had left for their long and famous journey. This is what I had told my host. I had happened to mention that journey. The trip to Europe. The idea of hockey versus the dratted ice hockey.

He had come here from Britain in 1969. He had read my books. He thought we'd be kindred spirits, bred of the same bone. And he said, "My good God man — that sounds a bit nationalistic."

It wasn't so much Trail, it was the World Juniors. I was talking about their fight against the Russians at suppertime.

"Didya see when the lad from Big Cove smucked the Russian in the head — set him on his ass?" I asked.

He looked at me as if I might be rather subhuman.

Well, it wasn't so much the World Juniors — it was Team Canada. It was the Summit Series of '72. It was —

"Good God man. I thought you were a novelist," he said.

"Novelist shmovelist —" I said.

So here I was outside waiting, as the snow poured down out of the gloom. But it was too late to turn back.

After an hour I saw the headlights of my friend's compact car coming down the street.

My heart leaped with joy. And in I got.

We turned about and started back into the gloomy night, the windshield wipers on high and visibility almost zero. And besides that my ears popping off every time we went up and down a hill.

"What happened?" he said, finally. "Didn't the reading go as planned?"

"No no — it went all right — for a stormy night. Some showed up — well three or four snowshoed in. I gave a pretty good reading — got to know them all on a first-name basis."

(silence)

"Well — what was the problem?"

"An age old problem," I said seriously.

"Oh yes," he said, looking at me and not understanding, "an age old problem." He smiled gently. "What age old problem is that, David?"

(I know when people finally address me as "David" I am about to make a fool of myself. That I have once again crossed the line from rational human being to something else. So I knew I had to answer him as impassioned and as sincerely as possible. So he would know he had not risked his life for nothing.)

"That son of a bitch doesn't like hockey," I said.

I began to think then that I would go back home, to my childhood home, and see the place again where we went sliding. Where we played hockey on the river. I would make the pilgrimage, for it had to be made.

I would smell the flat ice and the smoke over the dark, stunted trees again. I would visit the place where Michael grew up, and poor Tobias, and see the old lanes we all played road hockey on. Paul and Stafford and Darren and all of us.

But they would be ghosts to me now. Almost everyone was gone. The laughter against the frigid, blue skies would have all disappeared, evaporated like the slush under our boots in 1961.

I found myself somewhere in Northern Ontario, later in the month. I forget the name of the town. It was one of those reading tours where somehow you no longer know where you are.

Again I was billeted. The woman kept a bed-and-breakfast of some kind. I was given a small room at the back of the house. There was a hockey game that night. I don't remember who was playing — it may have been Montreal. It may have been Edmonton. It may have been anyone.

I could hear, far away, the shouts of the crowd, the sound of the announcer. And I left my room and began to look for the TV.

The woman met me in the kitchen.

"Are you hungry?"

"No — I can hear a game coming from somewhere — I just thought someone might be watching it."

"Oh," the woman said. "That's Burl."

"Burl?"

"My husband," she said. "We don't live together anymore — he lives downstairs and I live upstairs. He's downstairs."

"Oh," I said. "Downstairs."

"So if you want to go on downstairs and watch the game — "

"Well — I don't want to intrude."

"Burl? Intrude on Burl? Burl don't mind."

I went back into my room and sat on the edge of the bed fidgeting. There was a great roar. Perhaps Roy had made a fantabulous save. Maybe Burl wouldn't mind.

The wind howled. I could see a streetlight far away from the small window next to my bed.

Things in hockey were changing every day. Canadians and Russians were now playing on the same lines, in arenas all across the United States. The two greatest Canada Cups had already taken place — and within six years it would be called "the World Cup." (I didn't know that then of course.)

Everything was changing. But not so much for *our* bene-fit — yet we pretended that it was. We still pretended that the

NHL was ours. It was always one way to get along. That's what Canadians were like.

Suddenly I felt nostalgic. It would be good to catch the last few periods of a game. I left my room, opened the basement door and tiptoed down.

Then I caught myself. What would I do if I was sitting watching a hockey game and a stranger came tiptoeing around the corner?

I knocked on the side of the wall. No one answered. I hesitated and then walked into the room.

Sideways to me was a man, sitting on the leather couch in his underwear, with a pint of beer between his legs, staring at the television.

"G'day?"

I thought he looked over at me, and nodded.

So I sat down on the chair near the couch and began to watch the game.

It seemed as if Burl had been relegated to a kind of subterranean prison life. There were no windows in the basement, but he had curtains up. He had a huge bar, with two barstools, and a clock that told the time backwards. Above the bar was a picture of himself with a tiny bass, and under the picture his signature, and the words *bass master*. In the picture he was smiling as if he knew in his heart he wasn't a real bass master.

I was beginning to get comfortable. It seemed as if Burl and I would get along.

Suddenly something happened in the game, and we both started yelling at the television. Then roared at the obvious cheap shot someone made.

Burl shook his head. I shook my head. Burl got up and went to the fridge and taking out a beer, opened it. He turned about and started back. I was watching the television and grinning. Suddenly, he stopped. He turned. He looked down. He stared at me as if he had never seen me before.

"Who the Christ are you?"

"David," I said.

"David — David who? — what are you doing here?"

"You know — watching the game here — if you don't mind?"

"Where in hell are you from?"

"The Maritimes —"

"The *Maritimes* — what in the living name of God gives you the right to travel up from the Maritimes?"

"I don't know —"

I began to get a little flustered. He was standing in his underwear with a pint of Molson, and his little bass master photograph on the wall. He turned about, and there in his chair was a man from the Maritimes watching the game.

However, he could understand one thing. He could understand *why* I wanted to watch it. It was only a shock initially because I was watching it in *his* house.

Once I explained why that had to be, he was satisfied. Although, he did not offer me a beer.

Later, I even got to talk about my feelings on the game. How there are two *theirs* in the game, and how *our* game doesn't seem to count anymore. How one *their* is the product of business interests in the States — how we think it is *their* game; and how the second *their* is one that is strangely joined to the first *their*. The second *their* is the European *their*. How European ice hockey is supposedly more *moral* and *refined* then *our game* is. How we need European ice hockey to teach us a lesson. And that both of these *theirs* are linked in trying to defeat the *our* in hockey.

How probably this has already been done. How the huge arenas in the States and the lack of hockey in Hamilton attest to this, more than any of the false promises, or our pretence of still controlling our game does.

Maybe he didn't understand what I said. But he probably did. He probably already knew all of what I was saying before I said it. He understood Henderson's goal and what it meant. He understood when I spoke about my childhood friends, Michael and Tobias, and Stafford, and the game we played on the river in 1961. Because he himself had played those games too.

And of course I always spoke of Stafford Foley when I spoke of hockey. I thought of him on September 28, 1972. I thought of him twenty years later to the day.

September 28, 1992, I was at home in Saint John watching the news when they announced the anniversary of Henderson's goal. It put the hosts at a loss. They did not know how to approach it — as a human interest story or a noteworthy date in history. Finally it seemed that the best way to acknowledge to their audience that it was an anniversary of perhaps the most famous goal ever scored by a Canadian was to be whimsical and remote about its significance.

They laughed as if they didn't want to be known as the ones to credit this as serious historical information. What relevance would Canadians attach to it "now"? one of the announcers asked. And then added that her sport was baseball. You see, she was only pretending to be indifferent. But no one is indifferent to hockey in our country, and so it was a self congratulatory indifference — one that looked out at her audience and said, "I have risen above the game you wish me to celebrate as mine."

Without a doubt in my mind, the franchises in the United States need this reaction from us to exist. If they did not have it — if it was for one moment decided that the game was ours — there would be no lights on in St. Louis before there were lights on at Copps Colosseum. Winnipeg would not be going the way of Quebec.

It was 1984 and I was writer-in-residence at a university in New Brunswick. The Canada Cup was on. The night before, Team Canada had beaten the Russians in overtime to advance to the finals.

In the former Soviet Union, the game against the Russians

was on tape delay. All night, all day long, the phone was ringing at the Canadian Embassy in Moscow to ask what the final score was, who won the game. I knew who had won the game. I had watched it live. I wanted to celebrate. I wanted to talk about how exciting it was. I knew no one in Fredericton, however, except for certain English professors. And, as admirable as English professors tend to be, they were a different breed than I.

I went into the common room and poured myself a coffee and sat down — waiting for the arrival of someone to talk to. A young female professor from Newcastle Creek entered the room. She was a nice lady, and had met me once at the president's house. She'd once made the remark that she didn't see how anyone would be able to live without reading Henry James.

As she sat there I glanced at her. *Go on*, I said to myself, *Ask her — she's from Newcastle Creek — Newcastle Creek for God's sake. She'd have cut her teeth on hockey.*

I made a stab at my coffee with a stir-stick and looked about. Twice I went to the door and looked down the hall to see if anyone else was coming.

Finally I could stand it no longer. Turning to her I ventured, "Did you see the game last night?"

"Pardon?"

"Did you see the hockey game?"

"We don't have a television," she said.

"Oh, what's wrong?" I said. "Is it broken?"

Then I thought that maybe she and her husband had a fight over a program and someone had thrown the television through the wall — I know people who do that, so I thought — well she was from Newcastle Creek, so I'd better be discreet.

"We don't approve of television," she said.

There was an awkward silence.

I looked about, mumbled something to myself. "Right in front of the net — they score."

I too was from New Brunswick, I too had cut my teeth on hockey. I too remember sitting in front of an ancient black-and-white television watching the small figures of men gliding up and down the ice. I remembered the Richard riot, and how even then I thought it was ugly.

But I had entered, for the first time, another realm, where a woman from Newcastle Creek who may or may not have grown up on salt cod and moose meat could tell me that she disapproved of television and not be a fundamentalist. Could tell me that I wasn't alive until I read Henry James and believe it.

"My husband was up early — to listen to the radio so he could hear the score," she said.

"Oh," I said. I smiled. I had misjudged her. Forever I would be sorry for it.

"Yes," I said. "Did he find out?"

"Yes — he's heartbroken."

"No," I said, "not heartbroken — we won — Canada won 3–2."

She looked at me, as if I really was such a country bumpkin. And I suppose when considering it, I have been looked at like this almost all my life over something or other.

"But we were going for the Russians," she said.

"No," I said.

I had the same tone as a man might who had just learned that the *Titanic* had sunk or Passchendaele had cost us thousands of men for 50 yards of mud.

Hearing my tone, the tone of a person bleeding, maybe she felt as if she had won a moral victory.

"Well, we both hate Gretzky you see." Her accent now turned slightly British.

"Why?"

"Oh, he's just such a Canadian." She smiled.

"You hate greatness or just Canadian greatness?" I asked.

In a way, Canadians have been asking this question all of their lives. And while asking this question they have been running to outsiders for the answer.

In a way my learned friend's stance embodies the notion of the intelligentsia that hockey is a part of what is wrong with our country.

Of course I know this about my country. I have known it since Stafford Foley used to debate the merits of Alex Delvecchio in a room at the tavern, as if he could turn back the clock and make, with the original six, everything right with the world again and with himself.

It was, by some rascals, rather smart-alecky to cheer for the Russians. I remember this all too well.

It was December 31, 1975 — all day I waited. Red Army was playing Montreal. I was in Victoria with an acquaintance. He was extremely adept (or he thought he was) at taking the opposite position — the educated, therefore contrived, outrageous part. And so he "wished" to cheer for the Russians. He felt *no one else* would be doing this. (He would only have to listen to one CBC commentary to realize how Canadians bent over backwards to kiss the Russian behinds in order to be fair.)

I shouted at him, told him if he had only known the dozens of minutes of unrecognizable penalties that were given to our amateurs in Sweden and Czechoslovakia over the years he'd feel different. Or if he had only known the hundreds of thousands of dollars that Hockey Canada had given to the Russians to help their sport, he may change his mind.

He stared at me, as if I had not just said something wrong. It went well beyond this. It was as if I had demonstrated the kind of unfair sportsmanship he was ridiculing. "My Good God man — get a hold of yourself; it's only a game — you're frightening the house guests."

What was under attack was simply fear of a lack of Canadian identity. And he, a learned man whose father was a poet, connected to a university, did not wish to have anything to do with the sport that could make us feel — even manhandle us into feeling — Canadian. It was supposed to be done another way; I suppose a more *civilized* way. (Also it was the elitist idea that the ideal of Soviet life was one that hinged on working-class fairness.)

For most people who talk this polemic against hockey as a point of identity there is a certain degree of cant, of wrong-headedness. Besides, part of this kind of conceit hinges on the identity crisis itself. Because some of us continue to believe that Canadians are famous for nothing except hockey. There-fore they argue that Canadians must be greater than what they are famous for.

My answer to that has always been yes and no. And hockey, when you know what it says about us as a people, proves it.

So we sat in silence, he and I, in a little room on that long ago New Year's Eve. Montreal did not win that game as we all know. They tied Red Army 3−3, after outplaying them and outshooting them by a margin of 4−1. Tretiak, who the Czechs always seemed mystified by our inability to score against, saved them — and Dryden was in net for us.

Dryden never played that well against the Soviets, but all in all, well enough.

I remember at one point during that game Guy Lafleur stickhandling at centre ice, and mystifying three Russian play-ers. It comes back to me time and again when I am lectured, usually by university professors, on how the Europeans taught us finesse, and how shameful I am not to record that. I will and do record the Russians' greatness. But, my son, they did not teach us finesse.

Finesse in the age of Orr and Lafleur?

Finesse in the age of Lemieux and Gretzky? In the age of Savard (Denis) or a hundred others?

I was in Australia in 1993, at a literary festival. It is a wonderful country and has a rugby league and Australian rules. In some way (this is exaggerated) the difference between these two kinds of rugby is the same as the difference between ice hockey and hockey.

I was sitting with a writer from the Czech Republic and a woman who worked for Penguin Books. The writer from the Czech Republic and I had an interesting conversation about Australia and how it compared to our countries. All of a sudden he gave a start, and he said, "Oh — you are *Canadian* — I thought you were an American — so mister Canadianman tell me — who is the greatest hockey player in the world today?"

"Gretzky or Lemieux — I'm not sure which," I replied.

"Gretzky or Lemieux — Gretzky or Lemieux — bahhh! What about Jagr — ?"

"Who?" the young woman from Penguin asked.

"Jagr — Jagr — the greatest to ever exist."

"Great, no doubt," I said. "Definitely a great asset to the Penguins — but not the greatest who ever lived — he isn't even the greatest of his era — he isn't even the greatest for the Penguins."

"Pardon me?" the woman from Penguin said.

"The Penguins would be nothing without him," my Czech acquaintance said.

"I agree — he is great — but Lemieux is far greater — anyway the Penguins might get rid of them both within the next few years. I am very cynical about it."

"Who are they?" the woman from Penguin said.

She made a stab. "So what do you think of Kundera?" she said to the Czech gentleman after a moment's silence.

"Kundera — what team does he play for?" the Czech writer asked, and winked my way.

The sales representative from Penguin excused herself and did not come back to the table. Her meal got cold. This is true, and I feel badly about this now (a little).

Earlier that day in Melbourne, I needed a pair of shoes for this particular dinner. I went with my wife and son to a shoe store near our hotel. In this store one of the salesmen was a young Russian immigrant. He was fairly new to his job, and new to Australia.

He told me that the one thing he missed was hockey. He mentioned Larionov and Fetisov — he asked me if Fetisov had retired. I was never a big fan of Fetisov (except when he got punched in the head by Clarke) but I understood that his hockey talk was more than a sales pitch. And even if it were only a sales pitch *it worked*. For how many customers could he have used it on in Melbourne?

Years before, in my home town I got drunk one night with a boxer off a Russian ship. We liked each other very much. We talked two things — hockey and boxing. The only thing I can say is that all through the evening this partisan Russian who lived fifteen miles from Leningrad never once mentioned hockey as "ice hockey."

Ah but the game is lost boys, the game is lost. To go on about it, at times, is like a farm boy kicking a dead horse to get up out of a puddle.

But still, some horses are worth a kick or two. And if it is good and even noble to have sport, and if hockey is *our* sport, and if we can make the claim that we play hockey better than any other country — if we can make that claim, without having to listen to apologies about why we made it — then who speaks for *us*, as a HOCKEY nation, when three-quarters of our NHL teams are in the states, and 324 of our players as well?

It is not America's fault, maybe not even ours. Perhaps it is just the nature of the economic beast. And a few years back — in the dark age of Mulroney, when we spoke about selling out our culture, what great ballet were we thinking of — what great ballet had we already let go?

I remember an American friend laughing when she asked where Canada got its baseball players. It was the year Toronto lost to Kansas City and it had put a scare into many Americans. In fact, this lady's hair stood on end the entire time I spoke to her.

I was in New Orleans for a reading tour when the lady asked me this. I stated, "They come from the States or Puerto Rico or the Dominican Republic I believe."

She burst out laughing.

The laugh was insulting. And I countered it. I told her that most NHL players were from Canada.

But she did not respond to this. For hockey had no meaning for her. She stared at me as if I was being flippant. I suppose I was. It has always been a part of my nature. Half pathologically shy, and half flippant. Even when I was little.

TWO

WE WERE ALL GOING TO make the NHL when I was ten or eleven.

In those years — long ago, the weather was always *more* than it is now. There was more of it — more snow, more ice, more sky — more wind.

More hockey.

We played from just after football season until cricket started sometime after Easter. We played cricket in our little town in the Maritimes or "kick the can" as we alluded to it. After we put away our waterlogged and mud-soaked hockey sticks. Behind us and down over the bank, the Miramichi River was breaking its ice and freeing itself from another winter. In the piles of disappearing snow, fragments of sticks and tape could be found.

The sun was warm and smoke rested on the fields and grasses.

At Easter, in my mind there always seemed to be a funeral. One year, 1961, just after Easter, there was the funeral of a man who was shot in Foley's Tire Garage, and everyone was excited about it. We were all friends of the Foley boys — there were seven of them. The oldest of them was Paul.

He was the boy who told me that when bigger boys go into the corner after the puck — or after the ball if it was road hockey — always watch and wait patiently just on the outside.

"You're too little," he said. And in a characteristically protective way that other children had with me, he added. "You're also lame. You *can't* use your left arm — so if you just wait, the puck will dribble out to you and you'll have a chance at a goal."

A goal. To score one goal was the height of my ambition.

But looking back, half of us playing, half of us who wanted nothing more than to play in the NHL — which was always to Maritimers somewhere else — were going to have at least as much problem as me. Being a Maritimer certainly had a little to do with it.

One of our goalies was a girl.

Another was a huge boy with fresh-pressed pants and the smell of holy water, who believed in Santa Claus until he was thirteen. He carried his books like a girl and was in school plays with my sister. "I am of the thespian family," he would say, because his mother had once played Catherine of Aragon.

The brother of my friend who cautioned me about going into the corner was a diabetic — Stafford Foley.

Stafford wore a Detroit sweater and in his entire life he never got outside Newcastle. He was a fanatical sports fan all his life.

Another boy, Michael, had all the talent in the world but did not own a pair of skates until he was twelve. And then only a broken-up, second-hand pair with the blades chipped that he got from a pile in the Foleys' basement.

That was the year Michael also became a rink rat and swept and shovelled snow from the nets during the big games.

There were others who could play fairly well — one I know had a tryout with Montreal and came home because his girl-friend phoned to tell him she couldn't stand to be without him. After a month she left him for someone else.

Another — Phillip Luff could skate like the wind and had the brain of a salamander, and ended up playing the bongos. Another, my brother, could think hockey as well as Don Cherry, but couldn't skate well enough to make the pros.

As we grew older we all went our various ways with hockey. It was strange to see boys who were on the ice in high school one year giving it all up to grow their hair long and smoke dope the next, saying, "Hey man — what's happenin'? Get on down, baby."

Of course some of them took up the puck later to play in the gentlemen leagues. (Sometimes the gentleman league on our river was enough to give you cardiac arrest.)

I know at least five people who might have made it to the NHL if they had disciplined themselves. Perhaps, too, and I say this without bitterness, if there had been proper scouts from the big teams here, or more credit was given to the

Maritimers themselves. There was the OHL and the Quebec Major Junior — in the Maritimes the boys graduated to Senior hockey and played to sell-out crowds for their home towns.

I don't know how many of us could have made it, but there were some of us who could but didn't. Perhaps they didn't have the breaks; perhaps they didn't have the heart. The real thing the OHL and Quebec Major Junior is, is a journey through hell, at seventeen years old, a thousand miles from home on a snowy road. One only has to talk to any-body who *has* played in those leagues; billeted in houses, travelling all night by bus or car, suffering the scorn of the coach, if he was just not quite good enough to know.

One time a friend told me of his hockey days over beer. He told me who he played against when he was voted most valuable player in the OHL.

"Why, all those lads are in the NHL," I said.

He nodded.

"You — you could have made it too."

He shrugged.

"There is no doubt in my mind," he said. "I could've played up there — "

"Well?"

"Well, what?"

"Well, why the hell aren't you up there?"

He looked at me very seriously, as if being a writer, I

would understand. "I fell in love with a woman — and I discovered Shakespeare."

"A plague upon both your houses," I said. "You owed it to us."

"What?"

"You owed it to us — to us — WE WHO COULD NEVER EVER DO IT."

We never called hockey "shinney" where I came from. I suppose there are a million things to call hockey and none of them right. But I don't remember ever hearing the word *shinney*. When, now and then, I hear up-to-the-moment CBC reporters talking about shinney — as if this is the name that will reduce hockey to its embryonic, to its pleasant and nostalgic centre — it leaves me cold.

And of course we NEVER EVER called it "ice hockey" — or "NORTH AMERICAN hockey." Let the Europeans and some Upper Canadians do so. All of these things are blasphemous to me.

And since I am writing this for Paul who told me to wait on the fringe of the boards (which, like others, I never did) and Stafford who wore his big Detroit sweater three times too large and went blind and had the kindest eyes of any child I have ever remembered. Since I am writing this for Michael, one more time, and for Ginette, who went off to a number of bad evenings and sad marriages, but played the nets for us because no one else would, I will not call it shinney or ice hockey either.

I will still say that in those days the NHL was ours too, even if we were in the Maritimes.

And even if none of us had a hope in blue hell of making it, there was a moment when we all — even Ginette Malefont — thought we would.

Our houses were a mixed bag. You took what you got. It was a neighbourhood half white collar and half industrial and at least a good part poor.

I grew up beside boys who never had a decent meal and whose mothers were last seen somewhere else. And next door our MP was grooming his sons for law and politics.

Our houses, whether they were large or almost falling down, were our houses as kids. We noticed differences, that was all.

I was reminded of Paul and Stafford Foley's house when I was in England. I read in a paper in London, about a football-mad family, who were kicked out of their flat. It was the seventh flat for this family in two years. Every one of the four children went for a different team, and every game there were chairs heaved and dishes broken. The neighbours constantly complained.

Only the mother, God bless her, tried to remain neutral. Pa was as bad as the kids, almost worse. He had his team's colours tattooed on his chest. They had a picture, standing beside the flat they'd just been evicted from, all smiles and furniture with their arms around one another, ready to go someplace else.

I mention this because playoffs in the Maritimes, and at the Foley house especially, were like that. Boots and coats and hats lying in the centre of the floor, TV trays all over the living room. Hockey games in the kitchen, with donuts for pucks.

Outside it was pitch dark and cold; for it was still cold back then, when our playoffs came. And seven Foley kids on the couch with a huge, naked, picture window looking out on the snowy street.

A wild schmozzle on the ice between Detroit and Montreal, and suddenly little Stafford jumping on top of his twin brother — a twin brother who towered over him — to strangle him. "This is from Gordie Howe, you bastard."

His brother, Darren, was the only boy who took a hockey stick to my head over a game of marbles. It was the biggest game I ever won — 16zees.

The rink we most played on was the Foleys' — a large, lumpy, whitish-coloured rink in their backyard, strung with lights from the small sprag pole at the side of their brick porch. I remember nights when twenty kids would be playing.

Some, like Stafford, would always be wearing their hockey colours, others would have their equipment on: kneepads and stockings, skating about, or walking over the ice like wobbly calves. Most of us would be wearing boots. Our nets were most often snow chunks at four feet wide and twenty feet apart — our goalies played the net with old brooms.

Somebody would always wind up for a slapshot with the new puck he had just gotten, with six kids standing in front of him.

"Watch it — ya just clocked Lippy in the side of the head," someone else would say.

However, the outside rinks we played on were always uncertain; the weather could change three times a day leaving us with no rink at all and eventually, if we were not playing in the Sinclair Rink on our Peewee or Bantam teams, we would end up on the road.

I have never partaken in a hockey game on the old road where there wasn't some great dipsy-doodling that would put many people in mind of Denis Savard.

Some nights, especially when Michael was in nets, no one could score; some nights, when Garth was in nets, everyone got a goal, except Stafford Foley and me.

There were always fights. I mean knock 'em down fights that would turn your blood cold. The twins always fought. Michael often had a great fight with his half-brother Tobias — the only black boy we knew — the only boy I ever knew to eat worms on a dare. (The mothers always said "Poor Tobias" when they heard that he had eaten worms.)

Tobias was fed more often than not at the Foleys' house. They always had room for one more. In fact, during all this time their mom was pregnant, and stopped bring pregnant one afternoon in 1968 and never got pregnant again. That seemed strangely a part of my hockey life as well.

Tobias and Michael would come to the hockey games with one taped-up stick and try to share it, which would erupt into a huge confrontation. There were always interruptions. Mothers called us in, or as soon as he got into the net Garth would get cold feet and say, "I'm going home my feet are fweezing."

"Yer not going home yet ya big fruit — stay and play."

"I don't play with name callers."

"Who called ya a name ya jessless big fruit."

If only we could have seen each other then — I think we looked like we were on the end of the world on that small road, pressed between dark-shingled, wooden houses, with their dim lights. To many it would seem so lonely — kids from nowhere in rubber boots with runny noses, sliding along chasing a puck from snowbank to snowbank in the dark.

Even back then "Hockey Night in Canada" came from places that seemed another world, or on another planet — places like Chicago and Detroit and New York — places that most of these children I am writing about never ever got a chance to ever see.

I don't remember ever *not* thinking something was a little wrong with us or with this: that is, the concept of six teams — four in the United States.

It did not matter to me, at least not much, that two of these American teams were lousy all through my childhood — that is, Boston and New York — which essentially left four teams, two Canadian and two American. (Of course, I constantly reminded people that they were all Canadian players.)

Nor did any of this matter to my cousin from Boston who, in January 1961, came on a hockey tournament to Canada, and did *not know* that there was an NHL or a team called the Boston Bruins.

That was the first indication to me, that "Hockey Night in Canada," was a night that wasn't shown to him. He had no idea that they showed hockey on television. There was something stinkingly wrong with this. But the fact that he did not know there was an NHL threw me for a loop.

I stared at him in incredulity. How could you lace up your skates with nowhere to go? At least I was going to the NHL — with a few turns of good luck. (One of the ideas was that they wouldn't see my left foot which was turned inward, and my left hand which was crippled.)

"Why are there four in the United States?" I asked Mr. Foley about that same time.

"Cause they got the money."

I don't remember why this struck me as not the absolute answer. My idea — and since my cousin did not know about the Boston Bruins or about the NHL, it seemed in a way to verify it for me — was that the LOVE of the game had to be everything.

In a way this has been the main pin of my hockey ideas ever since.

Also, there was something more subtle in my conversation

with my American cousin that winter day. It was the idea of two cultures sparring and emerging from this sparring with definitive national attitudes about themselves.

I *had not* told my American cousin that there *was* an NHL because I did not want to inflict *my* superior knowledge upon a visitor. I was too polite. I was a Canadian. It's this national trait that has helped sideline our hockey history I'm sure.

Because ten minutes later he came at me with this: "What is the greatest basketball team?" And I said truthfully, that I didn't know.

"The Harlem Globetrotters," he laughed. "Don't you guys know anything up here? Hockey is not as great a sport as baseball — it doesn't have the statistics," my cousin said sniffing. "Baseball is what everyone watches on television down home. Mickey Mantle, he earns more money than all the hockey players put together probably."

I'd heard of Mickey Mantle. I did not know what a statistic was.

And then he said, "Hockey will never be on TV."

I was in Toronto years later — about the same time I first saw Doug Gilmour live — having dinner with good friends of mine, an American and a Canadian. When they asked if I watched sports I told them that I loved to watch hockey.

My American friend said that she could not follow hockey because she never knew where the puck was. I didn't mind her saying this, for she had never watched a game in her life.

"No one does," the Canadian quipped. "It's poor TV

because no one can follow what's going on. That's why Canadians now love baseball."

Of course, that is about as untrue a statement as ever was made about *our* game. Anyone who knows hockey can tell instinctively what is happening on the ice — even away from the camera. You can tell an offside, or a two-line pass in the remotest blink of an eye — just as you can tell a real penalty from a make believe one. Even when Stafford Foley was almost blind, he could tell this.

But talking to my cousin in 1961, my eyes were being opened to the limits of our game once away from us, to the position of the game as related to spheres other than our own. My eyes were being opened not by light so much as by shiners.

I did not realize at the time that being Canadian was part of the reason why *our game* didn't exist on American networks. It seemed strange to me even then that so few people recognized this oddity or spoke about it as a major problem in Canadian identity.

However I was a Maritimer — and though I thought of hockey as our nation's great sport from the time I was ten — we were as ignored by Canada in the Maritimes, as we ever were by the United States. And it had been a long time since Halifax travelled west to Montreal to challenge for the Stanley Cup in the late 1890s.

Except for one show I can think of, "Don Messer's Jubilee," there was nothing on television in 1961 that had anything remotely to do with us, except hockey on Saturday nights. (Not that Don and the boys did either — except that my grandmother swore she saw her stolen fiddle being played by Don Messer in the early sixties. "There's my damn FIDDLE. It's Don — he stole my fiddle," she screamed one night. Also a fanatical wrestling fan, my grandmother loved sports in general and hockey in particular. When her husband, my stepgrandfather, remarried after her death, he married a woman who loved baseball.)

But to be a Maritimer was, in hockey as well as in accounts receivable, to feel somehow outside the marketplace. Just as Canada must feel now. From Hamilton to Quebec, Canadians are feeling now what we felt in New Brunswick all along.

In the Maritimes all our chances with hockey seemed elliptical and remote. Three-quarters of the people I knew who had even a slight chance of making the NHL, never got that chance. Today the personification of this is, I think, Andrew McKim skating his guts out against the Russians in the World Championships in Sweden. I'm glad we have him there — but I know where he would wish to be.

In the Maritimes there is a province called New Brunswick where I and McKim come from. When I was young it was hardly ever recognized anywhere else, even by other Maritimers.

As a matter of fact, when I once explained to a person from Nova Scotia that my father owned a business, he burst out laughing. How in the world could anyone *own* a business in New Brunswick?

It left us in a rather odd place in the Canadian experience. For instance, on CBC celebrations of Canada Day in 1967, the last year the Leafs won the Cup, we were the only province not mentioned. Honest to God, we waited all night to be mentioned. "For God's sake boys — mention that we exist — Ma did her hair."

What does this have to do with hockey? In a way, for my nation, everything. For how my nation views itself, and how it is viewed, is how *our* sport is viewed. Those of us who ignore how our nation is viewed are the ones who ignore how our sport is viewed. Those who ignore how *our* sport is viewed trivialize what is tragic about our nation.

A recent American documentary about the war in Holland in 1944 forgot that it was the Canadian First Army that the German Fifteenth surrendered to. When *Life* magazine did their 40th anniversary of World War II they forgot to mention that Canada even played a part.

Canadians on the CBC were upset. I understand the feeling.

As Canada is sometimes neglected by the States so the Maritimes are neglected by Canada, and New Brunswick is neglected by the Maritimes — and guess what is neglected by New Brunswick? The strange river, the Miramichi.

Well, that is where my brothers and friends played hockey and lost their teeth, and boys for generations went off to play for the Hardy or Allen or Alexander Cup. With nicknames like the Spitfire, Trapper, and the Mouse.

—·—

The Miramichi had some good hockey players. It even had a few great hockey players. My brother was eventually drafted by the Oakland Seals. (I was proud at the time, even though I felt it was kind of cheating to be drafted by an expansion team.)

I knew people from my generation who had tryouts for Montreal and Toronto — who "went up" as they said. I knew a few who actually made it; Greg Malone being one. I knew a lot more who didn't.

There is a story of a coach from the Gaspé telephoning a coach from the Miramichi and telling him that he had "just the player you need."

"He's great," the coach from the Gaspé said. "He'd have made it to the NHL by now, if it wasn't for his drinking problem."

"Hell," the coach from the Miramichi said, "I have twenty players who would have made it to the NHL if it wasn't for their drinking problem."

Stafford Foley used to sleepwalk. More than once my father, coming home from the theatre, would see him sitting on a stump down at the end of our street where we played road hockey, at eleven at night with his hockey stick. He would be staring out at the river sound asleep.

This was when he was playing in the Peewee League on the Snapdragons with me. We were on the third line, on defence, and he was better then I was. His sweater came down to the bumps his kneepads made. He was number 8.

Since we couldn't skate we were called "two stay-at-home defencemen" and I realized that my coach — who would some-day own a bar where Stafford and I would ruin what little health we had — actually wanted us to stay at home.

That is: go home and stay there.

"Come on now — you're guys that stay at home — stay at home — really you don't have to do anything."

Even at that age Stafford was beginning to have trouble with his eyes. They watered and he continued to wipe them with a handkerchief he had gotten from his grandmother.

When kids were coming down the ice on a breakaway, Stafford would haul out his handkerchief to wipe his eyes, stuff his handkerchief in his hockey pants and rush bravely towards them.

He would forget to take his insulin, or get upset with his brother and refuse to take it — because his twin brother, Darren, didn't have to.

"Don't touch him he'll go into a COMA," was a line shouted in unison by his older sisters, as they stood about the edges of the rink, dressed in their convent uniforms, all wearing button-up blouses and huge crosses.

Once Stafford began skating about the blueline like a wounded pigeon, quite oblivious to everyone else. And then he just fell flat on his face, and began to crawl towards the bench. As the years went by this became more noticeable.

That is, his drifting away from the real world, into the world of lack-of-insulin-induced dreams.

And I am positive Stafford once played road hockey with us sound asleep.

One February night, a year before the time of this book, the kids had gone home, and Tobias and Michael and I needed another player. And there he was, standing on the snowbank with his hockey stick, in his overcoat and slippers, watching us, as huge flakes of snow fell under the spots the streetlights made.

"There's Staff — he'll play," I said.

And out he came without a word.

After about fifteen minutes of going up and down the side of the road, chasing the ball over the rivulets of ice, shooting it better than I ever saw, he was rapped over the knuckles by Tobias.

He looked down at his hands. There was a strange pause. He looked at us as if we were alien to him. He looked at his hands again. "Jeepers," he said. "Why did you do that?"

He looked at his muddy bedroom slippers, and turning, he walked silently towards his house.

Hands and feet. Those are the two extremities that always seemed to get it. Every one of us almost always had our fingers falling off.

I came to Stafford's house one day. His snowy mittens were on the step, still frozen to his stick, like the mittens of the invisible man, and his small boots were sticking out the door as he crawled on his hands and knees towards the kitchen.

"My hands —" he whispered. "My hands — I can't move MY HANDS."

"Get to the water," his mother was saying. "Come in and close the door, darling, and get to the BUCKET OF WATER."

"MY FEET I can no longer feel — MY FEET."

Hockey is played in the cold, and a generation of movies from Hollywood that have influenced our outlook about ourselves has shown us that cold weather is something *abnormal*.

However we are the coldest country on earth. And everyone except the children want to deny it. Thousands of us froze our hands, our feet and our ears every day just walking to school. And where we went after school was to a cold rink to put on frozen skates to play hockey on ice.

So our hockey is evidence, to outsiders, of our coldness, and with our coldness, our abnormal lack of sophistication, etiquette and probably humour. As I say, a thousand movies have been made to reinforce the stereotypes we use against ourselves.

Hockey becomes a kind of verification for outsiders and for ourselves, of how Canadians hate to be labelled in the first place. "Ottawa: colder than Moscow and without the night life," the joke goes.

Contempt for ourselves is the axiom upon which so many of our country's asses sit. Except the children. Except the children like Stafford Foley.

The children frolic in the cold like little white bears. Know what the game means. There is a time in every child's life when he or she wants us to regain the game, to be recognized by everyone as the greatest hockey nation in the world.

But somehow as we grow older we're cynical, allowed to be talked out of it. Certainly we don't have the media — certainly not the film or magazine people — to let the world really know who the players in the NHL are.

In one article by United Press International published on April 28, 1995, both the Canadian and American teams going to the world hockey tournament were discussed. The Canadians were mentioned as a team awaiting reinforcements from the AHL. The Americans were said to be a team who this year were handcuffed because they didn't have the help of "their NHL Players."

Canadian children, sooner or later, learn to live with this prevarication. And this kind of misrepresentation has gotten broader, deeper-seated and more complex. It is not recognized as a lie. Or if it is, it is a lie recognized as madness to contest. A lie that relies on omission of pertinent information.

Of course, I am talking about the exercising of social control over our sport in the States, to cater to people other than ourselves. To make sure we as a nation don't speak too loud.

Numb fools that we were so long ago in the drizzle of a Thursday afternoon, with the pavement bearing and the rivulets of water washing down Buckley Avenue. Young numb fools we were, who knew all the players on all the teams, and knew them all to be Canadian — just as we knew George

Armstrong to be Indian — thought the expansion was coming East. But not that far east — not to London, England. Somewhere around Halifax, where the "baby Habs" were — maybe Moncton, the Hub city.

We knew the expansion was coming because of hints, from our grey television antennae that tilted above our roofs. Hints that there was something going on.

There were new architects of the game who distrusted other leagues, and wanted to consolidate their business interests. To the weak-brained like myself, that meant a franchise in Newcastle.

There were some 50,000 people on the Miramichi — if we took in all its outer reaches — from the last bell buoy near Esquiminac to the headwaters above Stanley. It was perfectly obvious to me that of the 50,000 people, 47,000 of them should be hockey lovers.

Of these 47,000 at least 30,000 would support a franchise, 25,000 could buy tickets. We could easily fill a rink with 18,000 every game — especially when we made the playoffs and were taking on Montreal. So it was settled.

If we needed a new rink — for our Sinclair Rink only held 1,200 spectators — Lord Beaverbrook was still alive. He owed us — whatever it was he owed us — so he could build us one.

And Stafford Foley and I, and others of our ilk, thought that this was not only plausible, but highly likely. A team would be coming to Newcastle, NB. We waited for the signs, from our television antennae under the grey November snows.

THREE

SOMETIMES I BELIEVED THAT the Americans were as much a part of me as the Canadians. And, really, maybe even more so. I went to all of John Wayne's movies, rejoiced at the *Alamo*, watched dozens of films where the Americans won the war — whatever war it was — listened to a hundred patriotic songs sung from Alabama to Illinois as if they were my songs.

Now and again I would listen to a song or see a movie or read an article where it would be brought home that I wasn't an American, that no matter if I dressed like an American, or if Stafford Foley ordered a man-eating snake from Virginia — which turned out to be rubber, just like most of his other dreams — there was some difference inherent in us.

Perhaps it came because in 1781 Washington and Adams decided they couldn't commit their troops to help the colonists — many of who considered themselves American and were considered by the British as American — in the large tract of land called Nova Scotia, which then included my province.

But perhaps it is something else. Perhaps there is an identifiable authenticity to us, just as there is to being an American, that precludes being anything else. It isn't that we lack something, as is at times suggested, but that we *have* something. Not better nor worse, but something else — something different.

William Faulkner noticed it, when he wrote in 1955 a column on hockey for *Sports Illustrated*. He noticed, as people sometimes notice about Faulkner's work itself, that the confusion of hockey became grace, the seeming violence became wonderful poetic balance and movement quite unlike anything else. The contortions were really a dance, fast and beautiful, like great ballet. He commented about the number of women at the game, and seemed surprised.

I would not be. Women have loved hockey as much as any other sport, and would know it as well too. One only has to watch our Women's World Hockey champions to comment that they are undeniably Canadian — as Tolstoy once commented about Natasha's dance at the hunting lodge being undeniably Russian in *War and Peace*.

But there is another interesting note about Faulkner's column. Why did he write it at all? I have thought about this. Of course Faulkner probably wrote it because he needed the money. And *Sports Illustrated* was interested that he do it because he was a Nobel and Pulitzer Prize winning novelist. But the title on the article read: "An Innocent at Rinkside."

And the article is filled with the "ideas" of hockey that those who don't know hockey have. Hockey is violent and a throwback to gladiatorial contests like boxing. The article is worth something because Faulkner's perception about things makes him rise above the one dimensional view. But Faulkner's article exhibits something that it was meant to hide.

Articles on hockey in mainstream sports magazines in the States up until the late eighties were not so often done because of a *love* for the game, but were done to *sell* the game. Therefore they were all innocents at rinkside. It is a Northern game, a violent game, and (though they don't know this really bothers them) a Canadian game. And in a way, the game is beneath them. They might be asked to understand it — as Faulkner tries to ask — but few are asked to love it. (Faulkner wrote this article the last year Detroit won the Stanley Cup.)

Just as my cousin from Boston had never heard of the Boston Bruins, he could not understand my love of hockey. But, and more power to him, he did not understand my concern that he did not himself love it.

He was a baseball fan, a basketball fan, for his country owned them. For me, my country's sport was played somewhere else. I wanted them to understand that it was my sport.

Yet it was, as Casey Stengel sniped, the only thing Canada was good for — and my cousin did not have to love anything about it. And as soon as my cousin loved it, which came for him with Bobby Orr, he could easily claim it as his.

This is what Faulkner's article actually says. We own it, so we should try to love it.

In the late fall of long ago, of 1960 when we were all running up and down the outdoor rink, in huge boots, or pavement-dulled skates, in bare heads and kneepads, and a few with helmets that were pulled down over their toque, with ice on our sticks, the sport was Stafford Foley's and mine.

Stafford Foley actually believed we — he and I — would be elevated to the Peewee All-Star team, go on the road trips — one was to Boston like the Bantam As — and be normal, like the other kids. In my dreams Stafford Foley and I had already made it. Already had scored the winning goals in Boston — there had to be two winning goals; one for him and one for me.

That he was growing blind, and wiped his eyes with a handkerchief in order to see who was on a breakaway, did not deter him. That I had only use of one arm and couldn't skate — especially backwards — did not deter me either, in my dreams.

Each day he and I waited for the coach to make the final cuts. But each day the coach looked at us, and said, "It's still cloudy boys."

Cloudy was good. As long as it was cloudy that meant we still had a chance. It was when it was no longer cloudy — that's when you got the sick feeling in the pit of your stomach.

"Well it's still cloudy," I said to Stafford. "That means we have a chance."

However my own father was hinting that I should retire from the sport. One day he took me out to the garage and said, "Lift that brick with your right hand."

I lifted it over my head.

"Lift that brick with your left hand."

I could hardly get my fingers over it.

My father then explained to me that I was like a great hockey player who had suffered an injury. I was on the disabled list.

He said the "disabled list" because at that time I would fly into a fury — almost froth at the mouth — if anyone said I was disabled. But he knew that. And so, staring at me, he said, "You're not at all disabled — it's just a disabled LIST."

My father really didn't care if I played hockey until I was 80 — or 90. Half the time he forgot that I was "disabled." He would watch me doing something — like drowning — and he would say, "What the Christ is wrong with you?" and then he would add, "oh right — well stop floundering — I'll come and get you."

But it was my mother. I played hockey so bad she wept. "We've got to make him stop —" she had told my father. "I hate to see it. I can't bear to watch him any more. He can — curl."

Even curling was on television in Canada — hockey and curling. I suppose that's like Australian Rules and Bowls in Australia.

I remember the old Sinclair Rink and the effect it had upon me. Stepping onto the ice, once the door was opened, while the overhead windows showed snowcast skies, and car lights were on at three o'clock in the afternoon.

There were great senior hockey games there, home of the old Miramichi Beavers. And let me tell you what I think the Sinclair Rink had — just as the Beaverbrook Rink had in Chatham and a dozen other rinks had and have across the Maritimes, as much as the new multimillion dollar arenas in St. Louis, or in Anaheim will ever have — tradition.

One Hardy Cup in the Miramichi, with people screaming their guts out for boys who grew up next door, is better to me than a Stanley Cup in Tampa Bay.

Tampa is where hockey is now. In 1960–61 it was still at the Sinclair Rink.

In order to get into the rink free, Michael worked as a rink rat from the time he was twelve. His teeth were gone from the time he was fourteen. He had a James Dean kind of haircut, without ever having heard of James Dean. Michael was a rebel, simply because of his poverty — he didn't have to not have a cause.

In the end he would have thought the movie, *Rebel Without a Cause*, filled with weaklings. He grew up to have pulphooks put through his hand while working a boat at the age of seventeen. What need he talk about the angst of being a teenager?

There was an incident that happened that year. The year Michael and Tobias had one stick between them. The year Michael was going to get his new skates.

Michael rarely played organized hockey — organized anything. They didn't have the money. He grew up in the truest sense alone. He never went to the Foleys' to eat as Tobias did, but I'm certain he didn't mind Tobias going. He would appear out of the shadows at the end of the lane after supper, with his jacket undone, and buttons missing off of his shirt, his overboots unzippered and flapping and torn, while sleet or snow hit his bared head. Poverty has a smell that has nothing to do with dirt. It has the smell of darkness, of evening, of leaves in the earth.

There was probably, as far as just natural talent, no better athlete in our neighbourhood. He had a natural strength and gracefulness.

He could pick up a stick and flick a ball twenty yards to hit a telephone pole in the distance.

My father and I gave a boy a drive home one night. He was a friend of mine. And as soon as we turned onto his road he asked to be let out of the car. We did not understand at the time, but of course now it is obvious — he didn't want us to see his house.

Michael's house was like this. When he came up to our road, he came up to quite a different world. There were streetlights and patios and garages. There must have been a roar inside him to wonder why. In his house, rats ran along the walls and there was a cot behind the stove where he slept. There probably were feelings in him even at that time that there was no way out.

But God he could play hockey. He would always make his own rink, down on the Miramichi River — make his own nets out of snow, and have his own hockey teams. Yet he never was on a trip, never made an All-Star team, though he was as good or better than any of the All-Stars.

Just before Christmas of that winter — the Christmas before the man was shot in Paul and Stafford's father's tire garage — the last year Stafford and I believed we had a chance to make the NHL, the year we were beginning to hear of changes coming, Michael won a hundred dollars on bingo one school night downtown.

A few days later it was cold. There was a slick of snow on the street, and the air had the feel of glazed icing and the smell of sulphur. I was walking along and met Ginette Malefont coming in my direction.

"It's great Michael won that money," I said (and why I always tried to sound grown-up with Ginette I didn't know at the time). "He can get his skates."

"Oh," Ginette said, "he's already run out and spent it."

"On what?"

"He bought Tobias winter boots and a new coat, and his grandmother a dress — I saw it, some nice."

It was about that same time Stafford and I found out we were not going to make the All-Star team, and go to Boston, and be heroes. It was expected by me — I think — although hope is such a strange commodity in human desire that perhaps I actually believed I was going to make it — even though I was on defence and couldn't skate backwards, nor forwards. And even though Stafford would have to have his sisters travel with the team, so they could yell out at certain moments, in unison, "Don't check him, he'll go into a coma."

One day we came into the rink, and saw that our names were missing from the shortened list — and that list, was our whole life, that afternoon. Stafford read the names over again, and again. But there was no mistaking it. There was nobody named Stafford on defence.

"Jeepers," Stafford said kicking his foot monotonously against the wall.

I knew that that meant I would curl — for the rest of my life. A curler. The only other sport that Canadians were the best in the world at, my mother said.

But for Stafford it meant something else.

Part Two

FOUR

SUCH A LONG TIME AGO, 1960; I sometimes forget how many movies I did see in our theatre on the other side of town. Randolph Scott, John Wayne, Rory Calhoun, Clark Gable, William Holden, Dan Duryea and, of course, the most American of them all, Jimmy Stewart, who had that kind of New England rage that passed for morality.

All of these actors played war heroes, cowboys or, as in the case of Jimmy Stewart and Clark Gable, sports heroes.

The sport was baseball or football.

I wanted to be an actor for a little while. The Newfoundland poet, Al Pittman, has a poem about leaving a theatre in a small village in Newfoundland and trying to find an urban setting so he can act out the drama he has just seen. We did that as well. Everyone in rural Canada must have done that at one time or another.

The sets were always just slightly south of us. And, of course, we related. Canadians are very good at "relating."

That's what the movies from America and Britain allowed us to do.

As a matter of fact, I wanted to become an actor that Christmas. I think that this was the *one* time in my life that I wanted to participate in a school activity.

They were putting on a play called *The Hold Out*. It was one of those one-act plays found by the drama teacher in an old musty book of one-act plays from the United States. I knew nothing about it.

Our school was a dark, aging, high-ceilinged place. Always I have tried to describe the peculiar aspect of oppression it fostered upon me. I have never managed it.

It had heavy, grey hallways and linoleum floors. Lord Beaverbrook had gone to this school in the 1890s.

And here I was, with Stafford, close to Christmas of 1960, standing at the door of Mrs. Grey asking if I could be in the school play.

Mrs. Grey got her actors from the top — the crème de la crème of scholars. We weren't the crème de la crème. We weren't even close to the crème de la crème.

She was writing in her attendance book when we went in on that grey afternoon in mid December. The remarkable thing about this is that I remember her as being as pleased with herself as any child of twelve when she said this: "Well well well well — are you two at the top?"

And that was it. Not only were Stafford and I not able to skate well enough to play hockey, we were too stupid to act.

"We could act better than any of them," said Stafford, who didn't care if he ever acted. And then he said something else. He said that on the day of the play, December 21st, he was going to *boo*. He would boo them off stage.

He also told me that the girls would be naked in the play. (They did wear pyjamas, and it was the first time I had ever seen a girl, other than my sister, in pyjamas.)

December 21st came. We filed into the auditorium class after class of boys and girls. I was sitting somewhere in the middle. From the sets and design of the costumes, the play might have taken place in 1930. Or perhaps 1960.

It was a play about a poor boy, played by John Sullivan who we all called John L. Sullivan, who would not join his friends or go out to play baseball. No one knew why. They teased and tormented him until a fatherly, moustached, philanthropist, played by Garth, rescued this poor boy at Christmas.

Garth made a moral speech to the small group sitting by the Christmas tree and called the boy forward. The speech was about the goodness of this child. The sacrifices this child made for his family — working to support his mother — that this child was the living, unrehearsed embodiment of Christmas day.

"It's all in here," Garth said sternly, to the audience, touching his breast with his hand. He then handed the boy a baseball glove, bat and ball, and said that from now on he would take care of this boy's poor sick mother. Then Garth turned to the audience and thrust his arms out wide — and the lights went down and a star shone, all proclaiming the spirit of Christmas.

When the lights went up, Garth was still standing there — all the children on stage with their heads bowed, John L. Sullivan wearing his glove and holding his bat against his shoulder, as if he knew what to do with it.

"Boooooo," came a voice from the back of the audience, "Booooooooooooooooo."

I bit down on a hard candy and broke a tooth filling. From December until mid-March of 1961 that tooth would plague me. My face would swell up like a bun, and on occasion I could only see out of one eye.

There was only one boo. Everyone else kept applauding, and Garth bowed, and finally the audience stood.

There is a mythology to the American sports person that we have long embraced — just as Mrs Grey's crème de la crème did in that play. Of course it is the sports person in general; they fire our imagination, even heighten our personality. Soccer is one example.

Yet the Americans have taken this concept of sports hero and have manifested it in a way in which it has never been done before. Sports is somehow synonomous with the grandeur of the concept of America as a whole.

I have thought of that play many times. The reflections I have about it are many and varied. I have seen many movies like it. It is about generosity. It is also about American generosity and baseball as a symbol of bravery, goodness and innocence. It was the present Mrs. Grey gave to us for Christmas.

This was something that Stafford and I knew, but couldn't quite put our finger on — their heroes are so often our heroes, their movies and plays so often performed here, that we sometimes get confused when shown the American flag on their sweaters or hockey helmets — or worse the Canadian flag on ours.

But, regarding hockey, it gives us a strange ultra schizophrenia that, like most schizophrenics, goes a long way to hide its sickness from others and itself.

The Canadian psyche is not wrong, it is just different. Some of our greatest moments have been in defeat rather than in victory (sometimes we do blush when we win).

For example, George Chuvalo loses to Mohammed Ali and is considered by Ali to be the toughest man he ever fought. He was pummelled and never knocked off his feet. He fought back in every round.

To fight back like this a man must love as much as he ever hated. That's one of the clues for my respect for boxers.

He never won the title himself, but might have won it against Terrell, except something happened — the judges. They awarded Terrell the decision.

A man I know, Yvon Durelle, knocked down Archie Moore three times in round one of their first fight. He lost in the eleventh round. If only the title fight had been held in New York, where the three-knockdown rule was in effect, instead of Montreal, he would have won the Light Heavyweight Championship of the World.

Archie Moore, who was knocked out by Rocky Marciano, says that no one ever hit him harder than Yvon Durelle. For all his trouble, Durelle carried us with him into that ring and held us spellbound, staring into the face of one of the greatest boxers who ever lived without batting an eye.

But Chuvalo being the toughest and Durelle being the hardest puncher doesn't translate into a world championship. Almost nothing in Canada does. But that's okay.

The thing is, most of us never worry about this. It is a part of our nature not to worry about things such as this. Our dichotomy is so often the dichotomy of wanting to place rather than win. And that in so many ways is because of our association with the States.

Our nation is often at its best when it is fighting for others. Other people's vision helps us tip the scales. Once Canadians have vision, a vision about what they have to do, they are a formidable force. On the ice, no one ever has to tell us why we are playing the Russians or the Swedes.

Hockey is where we've gotten it right.

Our country hosts the Olympics in 1976 in Montreal. We are the only country with the distinction of hosting the event and not winning a Gold Medal. Later in a movie starring Michael Douglas about the dreams of a long-distance runner who is looked upon as a loser until he finishes the race at Montreal, we are given in the movie what we did not actually win in real life. The Gold Medal. For once a movie that lies about us works in our favour.

Things are like that in our country.

We come 22nd in cross-country skiing. Or maybe 23rd. Snow doesn't seem to do us much good here. It just forces us into using anti-freeze.

Though we could beat the world at snowshoeing — even my mother-in-law at 70 could snowshoe rings around a rabbit — it is not an event in the Olympics. It won't be an event until some European can beat some European rabbit at it also. That seems to be the way it goes with us. Toboggan racing would be just as exciting as the luge and not as explicit. Crunch five of us all together wearing toques and mittens. I could sit in the middle.

Even I can throw an axe, but axe throwing and fly casting and kettle boiling are out at the summer games.

Somehow we permit ourselves the luxury of being a country without a face and allow others to tell us what face we should wear. Somehow we want it that way.

Hockey's where we finally got it right, but we're not allowed to tell anyone that we have. So what do we do within the National Hockey League, and within the international hockey community — we tilt the mirror until we are out of focus again. The camera angle always slightly belittles us. For years we sent to the Olympics or World Championships those who could not do what those we couldn't send could.

It is also strange that we have not made a movie about hockey where the camera angle gets us in focus. Perhaps it is the art form. Perhaps movies about sports like hockey and baseball, show them not to be childlike, but childish — *Slapshot* is a good example. And perhaps that is where the focus is turned. The TV movies made in Canada about hockey usually tend to want to show that hockey is a game without any fun; like our weather, it is dour. They seem to be written with an explanation that we too know the life here is horrible. That most find a hollow log as soon as we see a snowflake.

So most of us switch the channel. And watch movies about American sports heroes instead. American heroes, in whatever discipline, protest, demonstrate, and sign autographs for the world. They always, always go out to win. Their victories carry a moral authority. Their defeats, a lesson to us all.

Ali beats a Canadian on the road back into our hearts.

The old Mongoose defends the Light Heavyweight Championship by knocking out a boy from my river. If they are going to win, to be our heroes as well, they have to beat us in order to do it. They become the metaphor for what life can attain, and how the human spirit longs to attain it. To cheer against them is almost blasphemous at times.

In 1980 my first publisher phones to tell me that he is glad we received payment for my first novel from Russia before we beat them in hockey at the Olympics.

I tell him that we didn't beat them, the Americans did.

He tells me it is the same thing.

I tell him that it isn't and if he thinks for one second it is he should tell Mike Erusoni this.

He says that they did it for us.

Canada too shelters itself in the mythology.

At that same moment in Las Vegas a friend of mine is in a friendly argument with some sports fans who are telling him that America is the best hockey nation in the entire world. They have the Olympics to prove it. They have never heard of Lafleur. They have yet to hear of Gretzky. They yawn at the NHL. They have not heard a word about 1972, or the Canada Cup. In effect they do not know what a blueline is, or an offside. And they still will not by the 1992 Olympics.

Yet here is the mythology. The underdog, against the greatest team in the world — the Russian bear. The greatest team, the greatest players, the greatest passers and skaters who ever lived. The boys who have a system. The Americans need the Russians to be just that.

They need the Russians to be great, to be better than all the overpaid, overindulged pros. And they, a team of gutsy spirited boys from Boston and Minnesota, are about to take them on.

It is a wonderful, wondrous mythology. It is shown on television on Christmas day in 1982 in Bartibog, NB. Canadians join them with a booming voice. It's as if Jacques Lemaire had never come over the blueline and let his shot go into the top corner, as if Bobby Orr never skated end to end, dazzling the spectators. As if Esposito never mesmerized the Russians about their own net, turning about to score on that corner pass from Ellis.

To the United States, Canada is not considered enough of a foreign nation when they decide the outside world is a formidable opponent. So Canadian friends of mine sing the praise of the Russian system as well and long for the boys from Minnesota to beat them, and prove for *us* what freedom and grit can do.

When the movie about hockey is finally made, Canada plays no part. Truth here is always somehow beside the point.

During the Cold War, this setup between the Russians and Americans was where it was supposed to be. This was where the drama was in the American consciousness, whether it be swimming or basketball or hockey. Canadians as the greatest, as the best, as the most powerful, just got in the way of a good story line.

In that age — in the age of my youth — with all of those people I used to know, there was no campaign about childhood safety. No worry about going up the street alone. In that age Bobby Hull was still a kid, and just in the league. Or before him, when Rocket Richard was leading the Canadiens in their golden age, I went every day to get cookies from a woman five blocks away, like a mouse hooked on sugar water. Essentially my brother and I were out on our own at the time we were six. I knew drunks and prostitutes from the age of nine.

And so too did a host of other children, some of them gone away for good now. When we played hockey we played it on a street, where drunks would stop to watch us, weaving back and forth, looking like the next snowflake to hit them would crumple them to the ground. They would offer us money to chase their hats, which tumbled end over end down an ice-slicked road. Earlier than that, I would watch from my bedroom window at night as kids played road hockey, and stopped to let not the car but the coal horse go by.

The fear others had of drunks and prostitutes and physical life in general surprised me when I went off to university. The distrust of physical life is in part a distrust at a certain level about hockey and about Canadian life.

But back to that earlier age. It's not that mothers or fathers weren't concerned. Perhaps it was a different concern then. Without mocking it, the accent put upon safety was not as politically correct.

Like all truths there is a severity to it. Children did get hurt and drowned and killed. Once that winter of 1960–61 chasing a hockeyball Tobias slipped on a crust of snow, went sliding on his bum and brand new coat, disappeared over the bank and fell – 32 feet. "I'll get it," was the last thing we heard him say. And then, "OHHH – Ohhhh."

He was lucky enough not to fall over the embankment at its highest part — that would have put him right into the chimney of one of the oldest houses on the river. A little Santa without bearing gifts. But he fell to the left of the house, and landed safely in a clump of burdocks and snow.

"Did you get it?" Stafford asked, who couldn't see that he had fallen.

The house far below us, on the bank of the Miramichi River had escaped the great Miramichi fire. The night of the fire, in October 1825, they were waking a child about Tobias' age on the kitchen table — that is, about 20 or 30 years before they played the first hockey in Nova Scotia.

They had six altar candles set about him, at his feet and head. He was dressed in a slightly pre-Dickensian coat and tails, attired in small boots. The great Miramichi fire had chased his parents to the river where they spent the night, up to their necks, leaving the child to rest where he was.

In the morning when the fire was over they walked back to the house. The candles had burned into the table, like little black smudges. The little child was still as solemn and as quietly dead, his hands folded about his wooden beads.

The child had fallen over that embankment like Tobias, chasing a ball. He had fallen. And in knowing those who fell 130 years later we saw his face.

Once a boy named Rory flew through the air on a toboggan and landed in the middle of the river. A fall of 100 feet. When we ran up to him he was clutching the toboggan straps so maniacally that we couldn't pry him off.

We had to pick up the entire toboggan and carry him home. "That was pretty good —" he kept saying. "That was pretty darn good. Don't you think that was good — I think that's like the Olympics — that was pretty darn good."

Today a safety campaign might be headed: "Do you know where your children are?" and have us thinking somewhat dreadful thoughts about what might happen to our kids. Dreadful things do and did happen.

Back then, in that bygone age, when the super six played, when during the playoffs every year some new star came out of nowhere from a farm team to dazzle us all, we were all running along the tracks jumping the boxcars of a slow-moving freight.

In the middle of a road hockey game we could leave our sticks and gloves on the street, and begin to run after it, catching up to it as it slowed down for a turn. Out of breath, with Tobias behind us, or behind everyone, except Stafford Foley and I, our boots half untied, our two goalies watching us, as goalies sometimes watch a brawl from their nets, we would jump the boxcar's ladders and be carried along a mile.

Then just as the freight was picking up steam we would jump and roll down the hill laughing, with snow in our mouths and noses.

It would be strange for a mother to be asked if she knew where her little boy was, and say, "Yes, jumping boxcars — that crazy little kid — I told him if he falls he'll be cut in two, but will a ten year old listen?"

All winter we went to the Sinclair Rink. Or played at the Foleys'. Often Stafford Foley's mother would have to come out and break up our fights, or turn off the outside lights so we would finally wander home.

In the spring, on those warm days in mid-April, a stranger walking down one of our side streets might suddenly spy fifteen kids wandering about on the Miramichi River, on ice floes, with hockey sticks, looking like trapped penguins. Penguins wearing toques and mittens with chameleon-like grins on their faces, shooting snowballs off one another's backs, with sticks that curved like Stan Mikita's. The ice was breaking up; our rinks were melting and floating out to sea.

One Saturday we spent most of the afternoon trying to keep our rink intact. Of course, we weren't that far from shore, but still and all it was a good feat.

"Take your hockey sticks and everyone — PUSH the RINK TOGETHER — one, two, three — heave. Bring the centre line up here."

"Look at all them little fish under our rink."

"It's those fish — look at all those fish."

Unlike Penguins, we never did win the Stanley Cup. Unlike Penguins if we slipped, there was a better than average chance we would drown.

And then one day every year, about the time the playoffs were ending, we would stop playing hockey, turn our sticks into spears and begin to spear the tommycod under our ice. The breeze would be warming, our mittens would get soaked and we would not care. The sticks would be splinters, the pucks lost and chewed and hockey be done for another year.

Most of us would not eat the tommycod, but Michael and Tobias would take them home, ten tommycod tails sticking out of Tobias' pockets, with the sun warming the stones along the bank.

This was our *other* place to play hockey in the winter. We played hockey on the river. Mangled trees and alders grew along its side in the summer, and by fall, the trees stood stark against the greying snow.

Fires would be lit near the riverbank, and Michael, who considered the rink his, would be out every day after school sweeping it clean, the ice clear and blue beneath his boots.

After Christmas of 1960, the year Tobias got his new boots and his new coat, I began to help Michael with this rink, along with Ginette and Stafford.

FIVE

OUR RIVER IS LARGE. IT has a long history. When we lit a fire to warm ourselves, we were doing something that had been done for generations. When Michael talked about getting fish net for backing for the nets he was making, that was exactly how nets were first made in Nova Scotia about 30 or 40 years after that little boy died in 1825.

We were just specks on the river. Once Michael went skating on the skates he had gotten from the Foleys' basement and Stafford followed him. They were dots out in the middle of the river.

When they turned to come back the wind changed, and the fire got farther away. Stafford started to get sluggish, and said that it was a good time to sit down and have a rest.

"You can't have a rest here Staffy — you'll never wake up," Michael told him. Michael was wearing his jean jacket, with his shirt opened.

The air was dazzling cold and far away the sun was lighting

the tree line at twilight. Stafford's small bony legs got weak and he took out his handkerchief to wipe his eyes.

"Hey Mike —" he said.

"What?" Michael asked.

"I want to go to sleep."

Michael got behind Stafford and pushed him, but couldn't make it. Then he tried to pick him up. And by then Stafford looked as if he was play-acting. Whenever anything happened that made you realize how fragile and wonderous life was, Stafford looked like he was play-acting.

He sat down, and looked about, and Michael kept skating about him on his old broken skates wondering what to do. And then suddenly something happened that would not happen in too many other places in the world. A car came along.

"Need a lift?" Neddy Brown said, his old 1954 Chevy filled with children and a wife and a drunken grandpa. There they all were in the middle of the Miramichi River, Neddy out for a drive across the frozen ice.

So everyone made it back by nightfall. Ginette wouldn't leave the rink until she saw them coming, and ran to get more sticks for the fire. She couldn't leave anyone, Ginette, in her life.

On this river fires were always lit and kept burning by loved ones for loved ones. And that fire near our rink seemed to be like this. It burned when Michael was there alone shovelling the snow from it, after supper when the air was so splintered and cold that each breath pained.

It burned near us at night when the wind howled and there were only a few of us left flipping pucks or chunks of snow across a windswept, deserted rink. It was all so primitive I suppose — hockey, frozen hands, ice in your lungs and the fires burning here and there about the river.

Fires had burned when Wellington defeated Napoleon at Waterloo — when the house I mentioned where the child was waked was just being built — and fires had burned all along the river when Savastapol fell in the Crimean War in 1857.

In both those wars boys from the Miramichi had fought. By the time of the Crimean War my great great-uncle was a boy on the river, and his son was the first in my family to play hockey.

To try to *explain* this to my uncle, the father of my cousin from Boston, was a rather difficult feat. To explain hockey as being part of the natural world of my youth, and therefore essential to understanding a love of my country, seemed slightly pretentious. Still does.

I have travelled the world and have tried to explain that hockey is more than a game. That it is more than baseball. That it is the non-intellectual impulse for life. But my uncle didn't buy this. Why should he? At any rate when he came up to visit us that year just after New Year, I wasn't talking like this. I wasn't going about the house saying, "Hockey is the non-intellectual impulse for life."

Even then I suppose I wasn't that crazy. I didn't even know how to answer them about Mickey Mantle. And like a

Canadian to my American cousin I said that hockey was almost as good as baseball.

"Well, hockey is almost pretty near as good as baseball, maybe —" I said. "I mean, if it just wasn't so funny and cold — perhaps —" I queried.

And they both smiled indulgently at me, as if I really wanted to tell the truth but because of some misplaced national pride I couldn't.

My uncle from Boston was my first foil. He worked for Cotts beverages and travelled the Maritimes and Quebec, because he was bilingual.

I had been bragging a bit to his son. I finally confronted my cousin, after three days of listening to him brag about baseball. I told him about the NHL, and that when they played hockey in the States they had to come to Canada to get hockey players. "Like me," I added, sheepishly one night.

Of course my cousin didn't keep this conversation between boys, he went to tell the men. He needed and wanted some quick clarification.

My uncle told me that they played hockey everywhere. "Not just Canada," he said a little sadly at my xenophobia. I've heard this statement since, saturated with the same kind of sadness.

My uncle was the first who doled out information to me about the Russians and the Americans. "You should go see the Russians," my uncle told me, "and we Americans too."

"The Russians —" I said, fear welling up in my heart. I didn't want to hear from him what I was afraid he was about to say.

"They are the *real* champions," my uncle said. "And *we* Americans have good strong clubs as well. In fact, my son didn't want to tell you that *we* won the Gold at the Olympics last year. So I believe Canada is somewhere in *third* place now."

"We are — you did, they do," I said, my voice a skeletal remnant of what it once was. "You did — you have?"

"Of course we have very powerful strong clubs in the States. We won the Gold."

I had known it was *all* out there somewhere, beyond the woollen sweaters and the sweat, beyond the great moves of Jean Beliveau and Rocket Richard about the net, but I did not know they would bring it here to me. I was just a sad little boy. I tried to look even smaller than I was, and bowed my head a little to look melancholy.

But I was beginning to understand two things about hockey. One was this; that it was a far more political game than baseball, and that my love of it was national. That Cold War collaboration and national interests were at stake no one spoke about. And secondly that, because of this, even as children we were not, as childhood baseball lovers, safe in the delusion of the game.

"Oh I think if they played our pros — they would find out," my father said. But his voice was like mine — it was a little humble, worried and apologetic that I had bragged about Canada.

My uncle wiggled his toes in his socks, lit a cigar and said nothing, smoothing some lint off his huge pair of corduroy pants, a deliberate smoke ring disappearing above his balding head.

Worse.

You and I know it is always worse. It always gets worse. In everything. For instance I never thought Michael's cough could get any worse, and it did. I never thought some of those children I knew would be left alone to fend for themselves and that the very air would swallow them and their dreams together, and it did. I never knew fifteen of my friends would die before the age of twenty. I never in a million years thought we would *lose* against my cousin's team from Boston.

I wasn't on the team — I never was on any team. This was the bigger lads — the lads like my brother and Paul. They were Bantams for Christ sake. But when Boston skated out and did their warmup, they were huge. Lumbering skaters, but huge, well-padded boys with big bums, from another world.

Our gutless coach wanted to protest, saying they had sneaked some juveniles with them. But this was not the way it was done. The oldest, the Yanks said, was twelve — in American terms they were small — tiny really.

We would play the game.

Their centre men were about a foot taller than ours. Their hockey sweaters were fantastically gaudy — red and white and blue. They had huge American flags on their backs. They skated about as if they knew everyone was watching them, spoke little asides to each other, perhaps about democracy, I don't know, and stood still and moved the blades of their skates back and forth like pros.

When our team skated on the ice to do its warmup, it was as if a balloon of exhilaration had been deflated. Paul accidently hip-checked one of their players near the centre line, and went flying through the air and into the corner.

"I'm sorry — excuse me," their player said, helping him to his feet. Paul limped over to the bench trying to save face by looking like he had been hurt in the actual game.

In the stands all our mothers and fathers — ready to cheer our boys — looked at one another.

And our boys looked like they were about three feet tall. Some of our players were wearing different coloured stockings. And Darren Foley went over to the side to get a pin off of his sister. And of course at that time in our country we didn't really have a flag. Well the British Ensign, or we could have gone with the New Brunswick boat. (Honest to God, I've never been really sure what kind of boat it is. It looks like a cross between a Spanish galleon and a Roman slave ship.)

Our goalie during warmup was flipping about, like a pancake, going down on every shot trying to make fantabulous saves to impress everyone.

He slipped, hit his head on the crossbar and rolled about the ice for five minutes, whining in a disgusting manner at the top of his voice.

The trainer (he wasn't actually a trainer — just Mr. Comeau) went over to check the bump on his head. "It's a long way from yer heart," he kept saying.

Then they piped in the national anthems while everyone stood still. Everyone sang the American Anthem:
"OH SAY CAN YOU SEE —
THE BOMBS BUR-STING IN AIR
THAT OUR FLAG WAS STILL — THERE —"
Everyone cheered and roared and screamed.
Then came our Anthem.
" — oh Can-er-da — our home and natives in our land
on guard we go and stand"
We didn't play bad. We got around them now and again on the boards, and shot from the outside. But we often had to dump and when we dumped the puck or tried to muscle them on the boards we were in real trouble. A lot of times we outplayed them. But they would simply stand near the net and knock us down. Overall they didn't skate as well but they didn't have to.

They passed and then mowed us down at the blueline. If we tried to check them at the blueline boards they would simply hold us off.

My cousin was not a bad player and I began to notice him more as the game went along. Our families began to yell at their own kids to get out of the way when the Boston players started to come into our zone.

But our young lads stood there and took the hits for town pride. In those days it wasn't like it is today. No-one was dressed like a spaceman. You could still tell who people were. You could still tell it was your cousin getting the hell knocked out of him. It wasn't an exclusive sport then.

"Bobby, for Jesus sakes get out of the way."

But our players COULDN'T get out of the way. It was not in their nature to do so. It was like telling Bobby Orr with banged up knees to get out of the way. It ain't in his nature.

Our goalie actually started to play well. Instead of going down and flailing around he came out of the net to block the shots, as if posture didn't matter anymore and playing the game well did.

But every shot he let in came from well back. And then something happened. Call it the X factor or the Canadian-consciousness syndrome. Everyone knows what I am talking about.

At the beginning of the third period they had tired, and we weren't tired at all. They were sluggish. We began to get around their checks. And once we got shots on their net our side of the stands went wild.

We began to cheer because when first we were too sure of ourselves and thought we couldn't lose, we now realized something much greater was happening, and we were cheering our players for their guts alone. The momentum by the five-minute mark of the third period was in our favour and we were only one goal behind.

And then came what usually comes to Canadian teams. It might have been worse. It was after all a home town referee. We got five unanswered penalties in the third period.

The first penalty was a roughing call because a Boston player had fallen down just in the corner of Tuff's (our referee's) peripheral vision. The Boston player when he went sprawling threw his legs high into the air, and rolled over as if he had been shot.

"OHHHHHHHH," came the sound from the Boston crowd. "THAT'S NOT HOCKEYYYYYYYY."

Tuff skated, as if morally shaken by what his town had done.

"Two minutes," he yelled almost in panic.

My brother was given two minutes. The Boston player bent over, was helped to the bench by a crowd of his own players and then skated out to take the face-off, a look of suffering and noble determination on his face.

The play had not more than started when the whistle blew again. Players stood about wondering. Tuff skated backwards, pouting, and looking very grim. Then he went over and pointed to Darren Foley, who looked at him so incredulously you might have thought he had actually done something.

"What-what — what?"

The crowd began to boo. Yet this I think only increased the ref's utter determination to prove that though he lived his life in a town of deceit and lawlessness he himself was smirkingly fair-minded.

It was an accidental call. He hadn't meant to blow the whistle. I don't think he meant to blow it at all. It just blew. To this day I'm sure he never knew why. And so in his panic he took his own to task. And once started he couldn't stop. Has anyone ever seen this in hockey in Canada?

"You," he said, enraged at everyone, "in the box — "

"Me — what the hell did I do!"

"In the box," he said and he began to skate rapidly in a circle as if he wanted everyone to notice him, shaking his head up and down and pouting not unlike Benito Mussolini.

On the double penalty we went down two goals, but managed when my brother came out after their two-man power play to score short-handed, when Tony LeBlanc — who was actually a Peewee like Darren Foley, and even smaller than our Bantams, squeezed by two defencemen, scored, and was lifted into the air in the same way Lemieux lifted Gretzky after scoring against the Russians in 1987 (although Tony appreciated it more than Gretzky).

But it was not done yet. We could not mount much of an offence after this because every time we did we would be put in the box. And it was all because Tuff had blown the whistle accidently.

Tuff was in the throes of whistle-hungry madness and like the great fourteenth century plagues it would have to run its course. All Canadians understand this.

With less than a minute left we were still down one goal. The play was in our end. Our goalie stops the puck, and cranks his neck on the crossbar again, and suddenly, Tuff, with an insane moral gesture, awards us a penalty shot.

He put the puck on centre ice and gave the nod to the fastest, largest player on our team, Phillip Luff.

Phillip had all the tools in the world to play a great game of hockey, but hadn't the brain. He would end up becoming a bongo player, dress in a flowered shirt, wearing a headband to keep the brushcut out of his eyes.

Phillip started from behind his own goal without the puck and skated to centre ice where the puck was sitting. He had picked up an enormous amount of speed by this time. He was, in the parlance, a "skatin' fool."

At centre ice Phillip winds up and takes a slapshot.

It blisters by their goalie and hits the post.

"Damn," Phillip's father says, and begins to clap.

Phillip, grinning from ear to ear, skates off.

His father waves.

"Hi daddy," Phillip says, waving back.

Everyone sits at the bench with their head down.

It took me a year to get over that game against my cousin's team. When we lost the Canada Cup to the Russians in 1981 I refused to watch hockey (I cheated during the playoffs) until we won it back in 1984. This was somewhat how I felt back then in the early winter of 1961.

Or *worse*. I actually felt worse on both these occasions than I can ever describe. I felt like I was to feel after the *first* game in 1972. How can one describe it? How can one describe the feeling I had? Well I will tell you how it was.

Do you remember the battle of Cannae in 218 B.C.? Yes. It was just like that – 2,300 years can't erase how the Romans must have felt after Hannibal crushed their army at Cannae. When the Romans sent scouts out of Rome to see how the army did, and stragglers met them saying, "There is no army now."

It was a feeling just like that. There was an utter silence. The Yanks had beaten us. The Yanks who didn't even consider hockey a sport had come into our home town where hockey was eveything in the world and had beaten us.

Worse I had bragged to my cousin about the NHL and that when the NHL needed hockey players they came to Canada and got hockey players like me (stupid, stupid, stupid).

My cousin had scored the winning goal. They had all cheered him and lifted him up and hugged him and he received a trophy. He came home and handed the trophy to me, to let me feel it, once, before he whisked it away, winking and smiling.

Suddenly it occurred to me that I had grown a beard as I sat in the den. I had become a southern rebel in April of 1865. We all had beards, my brother, mother, father and I sitting about listening to the yanks talk.

"Boys you played a good game," my uncle said to my brother blowing smoke rings above his head. He couldn't help but smile, and he was so patient and kind to me. It was as if I was talking to some Federal cavalry officer who was allowing me to keep my horse because I would have to go back home to plow my field.

"We put up a good fight didn't we," I said, trying once again for that old delightful bravado I could exhibit at times.

"You fought all the way," he said.

You'll find in situations like this when the defeated boys want to talk the victors always want to change the subject. So suddenly my uncle was talking to my cousin about going home. Getting back to their lives, to his wife and children, being just an ordinary person again.

"Oh you don't have to go yet," my mother said, scratching her beard. My father too, smoothed his beard with his hand. My brother, wounded, his cheek bandaged, hobbled about in an old rebel stovepipe hat, right in front of my eyes, as snow, delicious Canadian snow, fell in the damnable darkness outside.

But if you are already on the outside then things don't matter. If you are never a part of the fraternity then what does it matter if the fraternity loses?

I don't think Michael felt like this, just as the Maritimes never felt like this towards Canada, yet I think this was the way Michael wished me to think he felt.

He was there that night, helping with the ice, when the whole town suffered, when even the streetlights flicking on in the brutal darkness flicked a Morse code message of defeat.

Yet he told Stafford that the game didn't matter to him,

or the subsequent games the Bantam As won because he, as perhaps the best, wasn't in on it.

We were going to have our own games, he said, and start our own league.

Long after we all were in bed for the night Michael was still out, downtown, walking about on slicked shoes, his hair already slicked back in the way he would keep it for the remainder of his life, cleaning up at the taxi stand for a dollar or, over at the rink sweeping the ice and under the benches. He would bring a senior's broken stick home, to mend for a game the next afternoon.

Later when in my old stupid head I finally realized that hockey at some level or perhaps all levels was a fraternity, that there were insiders and outsiders, I thought of Michael taping up a busted stick down near the fire that he lit in the middle of a January night.

At that same time, back in 1961, Mr. Norris was thinking of hockey in England's Wembley Stadium, and was thinking along with others in Detroit and New York, in Chicago and Boston, of hockey in the millions and millions of dollars. They had to get it out of and away from the hands of the Canadians first — and they knew this.

I suppose we all have different motives when it comes to hockey. As Michael worked at ten o'clock at night to get his hands on a busted stick, in what seemed to be the remotest corner of a remote country, others were thinking of multi-million dollar television syndication rights.

The only dream Michael had was to get enough hockey sticks for us to play. He would lie down at night thinking of how to smooth out a bump on our river.

Our river. My cousin didn't believe me when I told him that we did not have a swimming pool in our town. I did not tell him that our river, miles long and a mile wide would suffice, without chlorine, to dip your toe in.

I think our river back then was somewhat like our Canadian hockey talent pool; it *seemed* deep and endless. It had farm teams in its tributaries. It was "unlike" other rivers. It was still non-generic. That is, hockey was not like football, or baseball. Now it is more like these sports, or at least the owners want to *display* hockey as such.

And now my river is like other rivers. It is still a mystic river, but it is no longer endless. Its great pools have been cut down, and overfished. It has changed with the times, and swimming pools dot our landscape too.

Michael's hockey sticks, all collected over January of 1961, doled out to us all taped and glued, sawed down for small people by the master of improvisation, are as forgotten now in his generosity as the water that passed under our boots.

Some of us never told him we didn't need his kindness, we had our own sticks, for this kindness was all that he could afford.

I asked Paul years later about this. About the expansion, about hockey, about what hockey meant to him. Paul had become more philosophical. It no longer mattered to him as it once did. The fire burned not as bright. Like some of us he hardly watched a game any more. He was often out of the country. Yet he said hockey was now a *media event*. The game no longer had a mythology that the media *knew*. It had media that tried to *exclude* the mythology. And this had gone on since the late sixties.

Anything the owners did *not* want the game to say the game did *not* say. And the main thing the owners did not want the game to say was that it was *Canadian*.

They were trying to resuscitate it in the States and so media, or what the media said about it, mattered much more than mythology. The mythology of so much of the NHL, was a Canadian one foreign to both the owners and the media.

Any mythology was cheapened to accommodate the media. When hockey was mentioned on television programs like "Barney Miller," "Colombo," or "The Rockford Files," it was almost always satirized. The boys never fought to get tickets to a game, but always had a comment about those who would go.

Paul had become cynical about it. He had watched the attitude of the media towards it. And the problem was always the same — the media we thought was our media, we cheered it, laughed at it, and glorified it. Yet it was not ours, and the game was not theirs.

He told me about the interview of Canadian players by the ABC network before the winter games in Sarajevo in 1984.

ABC wanted to show their viewing audience that though Canadians still thought they were the best in the world they had not won a Gold in years. After they interviewed a Canadian player who said Canada was the greatest hockey nation, they mysteriously mentioned that Canada had not won Gold in years, and made no further comment or explanation. Then they spoke of how many Gold the Soviets had won.

It was as if nothing had to be explained to their audience about why, Paul said. It made us all seem like pathological delusionists, Paul said.

I told him that I thought sometimes we *were* pathological delusionists. That our entire country was filled with pathological delusionists. Talk about being boring or stuffy or uninteresting. We were the bravest and craziest, the most interesting country in the world. Each one of us was worth fifteen Laplanders.

We get out on a baseball mound in April, and play golf in the snow. Even my father was a pathological delusionist. He owned a drive-in theatre.

I shouldn't say "even" my father because he was the case supreme. Sometimes in late October, at the little drive-in in Bushville he'd be playing *Beach Blanket Bingo* and giving away free hot chocolate with an order of fish and chips. It was as if the poor bugger was going to make his fortune doing this.

Snow would be dawdling down, all the underpaid staff in long underwear, the projectionist in hat and gloves. Ginette, who worked for us faithfully, there making fish and chip boxes, and thawing out wieners.

But the worst of this is — cars actually start arriving.

Neddy Brown and his family, the grandpa as drunk as a snake, and Neddy wearing sunglasses in a cheap Elvis imitation jacket: "How ya doin — how ya doing tonight — are ya lonesome — lonesome tonight?"

This is true, I don't lie about things (or at least I don't like to get caught lying about things).

Paul said he knew it was all true and he believed me. "It was just like poor Stafford and his rubber snake," he said. "He kept trying to convince his brothers and sisters that it was real — tried to feed it mice — just like he tried to convince us that Gordie Howe phoned him up."

"Pathological delusionists," I said, a little sheepishly, because one day Gordie Howe actually *did* phone me up.

SIX

I T WAS, THAT DAY IN 1989, when I went back to visit the town and met Paul, as if we were finally beginning to recognize what and who we were. It was deep winter — one of those winter days when you either go to work or start to drink wine at seven in the morning. We were walking along the highway on our way to visit Stafford Foley.

I could see how Stafford, back in 1961, would think his snake was real. He would think it was real because he wanted it to be real. He didn't want to sleepwalk — walking down the street in his slippers. He didn't want to have insulin attacks, where he would become as strong as the Amazing Hulk, and five or six of us would have to hold him down and feed him a sugar cube. He didn't want to be tiny and blind. He wanted to have his own snake. He wanted to play hockey.

And if it wasn't going to happen he would become a pathological delusionist. He would tell people Gordie Howe phoned him or he was over talking to the coach — who wanted him to become a scout for the team. Stafford had all kinds of plans such as this, back in 1961, and he was no more deluded than most of us.

Not only did my father play *Beach Blanket Bingo* in October, where we would stand about in earmuffs watching our breath — and of course Annette — but, when I was not much older than this, we would have beach parties in January after a hockey game.

Yes we were all essentially madly self-deluded.

"But that is the fabric of our entire lives," Paul said. "Self-delusions, overcome by self-mockery."

"And others' mockery of us overcome by self-delusion."

Like Stafford and Michael. Like Phillip Luff's father who wanted Phillip so badly to become a great hockey player that even when Phillip was in his 30s he couldn't put away his skates. Even though his body was broken up and hurt, tormented by injury, he did not, for his father's sake give up the fantastic dream. Even though his father by then wanted him to, Phillip could not.

"Still delusion or no, there will always be great moments," Paul said, "great moments for us in hockey."

Hockey and other things as well. Mr. Foley played hockey in Europe on the army team from the North Shore. They played exhibition games in Scotland and England.

He was a great winger. Yet the greatest moment of Mr. Foley's life came on D-Day.

On D-Day Mr. Foley was doing the one thing that he didn't

quite expect to be doing. When the North Shore Regiment reached the wall, and skirted the first town, Mr. Foley had the opportunity to help deliver a baby girl, wrap it in swaddling clothes and keep on fighting.

Paul and Stafford knew this. And Mr. and Mrs. Foley could never ever turn anyone away from their door. Any child, any orphan was theirs. So, for that hockey year of 1961, was little Tobias.

I was once reprimanded by one of our new generation for thinking too much of children as orphans, or underprivileged little humans. Still and all, I knew my share of them. And I suppose as Mr. Foley thought, if you know one, you know them all. That is, orphans are like murderers. Once you know one, you can clue in to certain aspects of all of the others.

Murderers almost always smile as if you're the *one* they *wouldn't* kill, and orphans almost always smile as if you're the one they belong to. Both of them, like Canadians, can be self-deluded about their essential makeup.

Tobias used to attend all the birthday parties at the Foleys' and leave certain articles of clothing there, so he could come back at a later date to retrieve them. But at other birthday parties he was left out. Shamefully I don't remember him being invited to mine.

I remember a richer kid — one of the Griffin kids, showing Tobias and Michael his new goalie pads and skates and saying with smug certainty (as if he was repeating what his father had told him), "Kids like that always like to be shown what they are missing."

Tobias did like to see what other children had. And Stafford on more than one occasion complained to us that Tobias was in his bed upstairs sleeping. The first time I heard him complain I was at the door to get a glass of water after a game of road hockey.

"How can I work — how can I concentrate, how can I feed my snake — how can I make out my coach's report, how can I write in my hockey journal — if Tobias's sleeping up there?"

"Let him sleep," Mrs. Foley said. "I'll wake him up later."

"I wouldn't sleepwalk down to his house," Stafford would say. "I have a twin brother — who gets all the credit and is on the All-Star team, and now I have a person sleeping in my bed. It's as if — as if I don't exist — as if I'm — im-material."

I drank my water and listened to him.

He walked about the kitchen, with one strand of hair sticking up, and his hands in the pockets of his jeans.

The sad thing was Michael overheard this as well.

Stafford did have a point. His brothers went out to play on the All-Star team — Darren was so good he had been elevated to the Bantam As, and Stafford would sit in the stands with his sisters cheering and holding his handkerchief in his hand.

"Skate — skate," he would yell, or "Hit him — hit him — move, move."

But at times Stafford became very smug with me. I had to

pretend a lot. Stafford would talk to the coach, drive back and forth with his father and players to the big game, sit in the dressing room, look over somebody else's equipment. He *became* an essential part of the team without having much to do with it. To him I was just any other fan.

"They think he's me," his brother would complain to his mother. "He's going around taking credit for all my work."

"And who takes credit for all of my work," Stafford shot back, "I'm a scout for the team — I have responsibilities. I know every player on every team in the North Shore — and I have someone who has taken over my life, sleeps in my bed, borrows my puck, pats my mouse, borrows my stick, comes in for breakfast and sits at my place waiting for toast. I'm disappearing — slowly but surely, and I refuse to let that happen."

Stafford was essentially saying that Tobias was like Bette Davis's understudy in that movie and he was determined to fight back before the understudy got the leading role. Or like that girl in the story of the three bears.

On the other hand his twin brother, Darren, thought Stafford was the understudy trying to take over.

Mr. Foley drove them back and forth to the games, his face flushed from a drink or two of wine. Almost always he had a bottle or two of wine rolling about under the seat of the car.

On Sunday they would be at church, Tobias with them wandering behind them about three feet. They would receive communion, mumble their prayers, all go back to the same pew, all look saintly.

Then Stafford would go home, up to his room where he would go over the rosters of the other teams in the All-Star league; who was scoring, who was dangerous — in his notebooks the best players had an X beside them in red. This was in 1961, and at least four of these players either had tryouts with the NHL or made it into semi-pro by 1970. A few more could have made it, if the bottle didn't get to them.

Stafford knew the game of hockey. But like some he had a quirky knowledge. Like many Canadians it was out of his *heart* and *soul* instead of his mind. But still at the age of eleven, like thousands of other Canadians, he probably knew the game as well as Mr. Norris.

But it was a delusion on his part to think he was making the slightest difference in keeping a record for the Bantam As. In the North Shore Bantam As there were three teams we could beat, and two teams we couldn't. No amount of roster checking would improve this.

He would sit at his desk, his rubber snake in a cardboard box beside him, with its tin of water, his magnifying glass nearby.

Outside, one of those snowstorms that always came in our youth and stayed for months, fell. His house was one of those hard brick, two-storey ones with cement steps, in the middle of our neighbourhood. The halls were blank and wide and white. The windows rattled. One room was hot, the rest were cold. There were almost no books. Palm leaves from the last Palm Sunday still stuck into a picture of the Pope, and the kitchen was filled with coats and hats and boots and cookies with a bite or two taken out of them. In the cracked basement were eleven or twelve mismatched pairs of skates, hockey pads, goalie gloves, mitts, pucks covered in oil. This was where Michael's pair of skates had come from. Size seven on his right foot, size nine on his left.

It was a house, then, like a hundred others in our town. From the window across the hall you could see the sweep of the snow-packed Miramichi. Far away in Bushville, you could spy the dots of children on a rink — but this was not Michael's rink.

And in Stafford's room, which he shared with Paul and his twin, and lately Tobias, he sat at one of those small all-conforming, wooden desks and made out his report to the coach.

By the time he finished, Tobias would be asleep on his bed.

Tobias called sleeping in Stafford's bed, playing with Stafford. Stafford would walk about the room on his tiptoes so as not to wake him, as those dreary monotonous Sunday afternoons passed.

Only Michael became furious with Tobias over this. At times Michael's fury could reach out and try to crush his brother — half-brother really — blaming him for everything that went wrong. He hated Tobias at times, hated him with all the misery in his heart, hated him for following him to games, for having to share his sticks. Hated him for going to the Foleys'. But it was at the Foleys' where Tobias could sleep.

At four in the afternoon Stafford would wake him.

"Oh," Tobias would say, "I fell asleep."

Tobias got scared one afternoon when he woke and saw Stafford with a needle in his arm. "Don't worry," Stafford whispered, "I do this every day."

Tobias thought Stafford's house was the greatest house in the world, and Stafford the greatest person he had had the opportunity to meet. He couldn't believe anyone could be lucky enough to live there.

After dark, the snow still falling, over all the eastern world from the Gaspé to the Miramichi, covering the thousands of square miles, the small valleys and dark lonely bridges — after dark and after he had eaten his supper, Tobias left the Foley house and walked down to where the streetlights ended.

"I for one am not sorry to see him go — I have things to do — we're going to start a broomball league tonight at cubs —" And sniffing in unfelt derision, baseball cards in his pocket, with the players names scratched out and names like Delveccio written over them, Stafford would finally, pepper shaker in hand, sit down to his stew.

Tobias' grandmother, who was called his mother, was named Bert. She was a tough leather-necked, half-mad, old lady. No one knew where their fathers were or where their mother had gone. Bert's last name, like Tobias' was Kennedy, although Michael's name was LaGrim.

Bert would hobble about on her two canes from window to snowy window, place to place, watching for people to come up the ice-slicked path. The windows were covered in plastic to keep out the elements.

During Christmas she would wait for the turkey to arrive from the priest house, or wait for some minister from a strange, obscure church to come and talk, about Tobias.

Bert talked out of the side of her mouth, puffing a hand-rolled cigarette, and drinking homemade wine. I would come down some days to sit and wait for Michael.

Bert said there would be no man on the moon in her life time. "Crows will be flying arse-first across the Miramichi before they put a man on the moon," she told us one snowy afternoon in January, and then coughed up phlegm, until her face turned beet red, laughing, and hauling on her cigerette. She had the habit of chewing the loose tobacco with her teeth, and a tiny shred of white paper was always stuck to her lips.

I told my uncle about what she had said about the moon landing.

"Who told you?" he said.

"Old Mrs. Kennedy said it."

When Bert spoke Michael would sit in the corner, his eyes fixed on the old stove that heated most of the house, unflinching. He never disagreed with her.

Stafford and I were helping Michael make his nets. He was no carpenter, and he was worried about losing his whole plan of having a rink, and his own team, if he couldn't have the nets. He needed fish net, but the only one he had was one that an uncle of his had used to poach with. It was a four-inch gill, twisted and ripped. His uncle had drowned in it.

There were other things about Michael that winter. He was talked to by people we didn't know who sometimes came up that grey ice-slicked path those dark afternoons. The police had also questioned him about a break-in at the creamery.

He wanted to have nets like they had at the rink, but four-inch mesh was too large. You could put a puck right through it. Which Stafford and I immediately recognized as probably our only chance to score a goal.

Michael needed to be as delusional as Stafford and I, as Paul Foley, years later, said we all were.

"You were all delusional to think that hockey would behave well no matter how it was treated," Paul said. "Can the will ever be there to get back to the way it was? — only if it doesn't matter to others. Others have found a way to redefine it. And no-one can or should ever blame the players. They have to go to make a living.

"Where would you rather play — in Skunk Ridge like Phillip Luff or Chicago like Denis Savard? But still the players always know there are tradeoffs.

"But you see what has been done lately — and our media plays at least its part — during the amateur draft is to create a great dazzling world of the *auction block*. The principle idea invested in is this: that we as Proud Canadians are over-whelmed that a certain boy from Brandon or Sault Ste. Marie, is picked over someone from Sweden to go to Los Angeles. No longer do we even have a pretence of claiming it as ours. Nor should we. That is the shame of it."

He continued, "I will tell you how an uncle died, and you might relate it to Canadian hockey. He went into the hospi-tal, and the doctors and nurses joked with him and told him that he was doing fine. He believed the doctors. So he did not worry, until the pain got too severe.

"He went back to the hospital. The doctors re-evaluated and found that they had made a mistake with the first diag-nosis. In a strange way this was blamed on him. Hadn't he known the pain was severe?

"They told him that if he followed the proper precautions he would get better. So he entered the second stage of his ill-ness. But things had advanced by neglect, so that no matter what precautions he deteriorated and the illness advanced to the third stage. And it was in this third stage where his rel-atives, as the *audience*, began to see that no one was trying to cure him anymore. And once it was realized that nothing could be done, it was hoped that he would die as quickly as possible for his and everyone else's relief. This is what Canada is rushing towards now."

But how can you comprehend, in 1961, when you are trying to buy a puck, that they are talking about franchises in Los

Angeles? And that people, adults you looked up to, would be gulled into thinking that those franchises would be worth something to Canadians. That, to us, was where the real self-delusion lay; we only existed, with Michael skipping school two days a week to put his rink together, in the realm of the possible.

I would never say the game was greater back then, but no matter how much bigger and stronger the players are now, there was a harder edge to the game in 1961, along with an innocence. The Trail Smoke Eaters seemed to personify this, in a strange way that year.

Stafford was hoping and praying that Detroit would win the Stanley Cup in 1961. He was too young to remember when they won it in 1955. Most of the people on my side of the street were going for the Habs, although Rocket had just retired, and their dynasty was limping into the future.

There was Chicago. And the Leafs were on the horizon. They had people from the Toronto Marlboroughs who were coming into their own like Mahovlich. I hated the Million Dollar Baby until he went to Montreal.

I had strong dislikes. I hated Toronto. They were anti-Hab people. I never warmed to Chicago — I never warmed to Bobby Hull. But I went for any team playing Toronto. Just as today I go for any team that is playing against Boston. It is irrational, I know. My dislike for Boston started when they got their people — Espo, Orr, Sanderson, McKenzie and others — and my cousin in Boston finally started to claim them.

As if suddenly hockey had become *acceptable*. My uncle would telephone and you'd hear, "Heh heh heh heh heh."

I love Orr really. If I were to pick the three greatest players who ever lived I would be hard pressed not to include Orr, and I cannot help but think of and long for his brilliance. The rush where he picked up his glove, went around the net. His goal in St. Louis. I think he is the greatest defenceman who ever lived, perhaps the best player.

In 1961 Bobby Orr was still in the future playing somewhere in Ontario with a brushcut, but already the powers that be were looking at him.

Stafford and I were still thinking that they might be looking at us.

Michael was going to have his rink, one way or the other, but I didn't know why he went to such trouble. He was often fighting now, in school. Some of the boys were calling Tobias: "Nigger baby." And so Michael had to fight.

His cold **was** constant, his shirt was opened. Half the winter he wore shoes. He had the gentlest smile.

I sometimes forget how small we all were in baggy pants and frayed sweaters smelling of weather and wood smoke, and how he was as small as most of us, for he seemed to be grown up.

HOCKEY NIGHT IN CANADA

Hockey was synonymous with the Esso man, and the "Untouchables."

The Esso man came on during the commercial breaks, and his mild-mannered, enthusiastic pitch was either lauded or hated, depending if your team was winning or not. I just pretended, since we got our oil from the Irving man, that this was an Irving guy.

After the game — the three-star selection and the final Esso commercial — came the "Untouchables," with Elliot Ness.

It always seemed fitting that it took place in Chicago. Where Bobby Hull was. And it is still strange to think that during those 1930s Elliot Ness times, hockey took place there as well, with boys from the wheat fields of Manitoba playing.

So Saturday was our night. Even if you were beaten up out on the road during the day. Even if you had a puck in the side of the face, or were slashed, or disowned. After supper, the traffic would diminish, the streets become quiet, the sound of snow scuttling across them.

Michael and Tobias didn't have a television. They would leave their house after supper and make their way to different houses. Tobias would always go out first and Michael would follow about five minutes later.

Michael would stand outside, letting Tobias knock at our door, and then he would wait a moment and follow him inside. He would never sit down until he was asked, but would stand by the door.

They roamed not only our neighbourhood but others for

this privilege. Sometimes seen as far away as the neighbour-
hoods of Skytown, or Skunk Ridge.

Stafford thought he was a big wig travelling with the Bantam
A team, like some kind of club reporter. People said he had
bribed the coach, had his father give him new white-wall tires
at half price. Stafford never denied this, so maybe it was true.

But it was in that month of January, 1961, that another
rumour started. And Stafford Foley knew something. He
knew something that Michael knew.

With his half-blind eyes, he had seen the lie invested in
closer to home than I thought. He was like Max Schmelling,
who noticed when Louis dropped his left — he had seen
something. He had seen a half a dozen players who couldn't
even come close to Michael.

And what he had seen was this. The reason Michael was
not on the Bantam All-Star team was not because his skates
were no good, but because of his family. Five of the mothers
complained about who he was and had a private meeting with
the coach.

And it was this secret complaint that caused him to be cut,
and caused the coach a certain leniency with Stafford's travelling plans. And Michael pretended for Tobias' sake that he
did not know this.

Years later when people were doing a play of mine in
Sackville, when everyone was working together and when
there was a great sense of camaraderie with everyone, I

realized that this was how my brother, and Stafford's brothers, felt most of their young life, and what Stafford and I had missed.

And I knew why Michael was making his rink, down over the bank, by himself.

SEVEN

THE OLD COLONEL LIVED next door to us. At night the balls were always being whacked into his door or against his window, and he would run to get them and toss them back to us.

He had Michael shovel his driveway, and always came out to speak to us. Some nights he would stand in the cold for an hour in his T-shirt, his false teeth chattering a mile a minute.

He told us that the Europeans were playing hockey better and better. The Norwegians now had a Canadian coach, and the Swedes were big. That, during the war when the Canadians put on exhibitions in England, like Mr. Foley and the North Shore Regiment, we were pretty much top drawer. But he said, not any more. In fact he was reiterating what my uncle had said, but thankfully he wasn't as happy about it as my uncle was. The Russians were good — not as good as the pros yet, but soon would be — the Swedes were becoming stronger — the Czechs too.

Of course we had all heard of this, and were immediately suspicious.

"Well if we send our pros over, " I told the old Colonel, "That would put a surprise into them. We'd do them in."

I was just saying what I had heard, just repeating it for hope sake. Feeling like a kid trying to save the whole world. It can't be done.

The old Colonel smiled at me. "They are very good," he said to me and there was a twinge of regret in his voice. "I think our pros can and will beat them — and maybe always will be able to — if only our pros remain ours."

The Colonel had lived his life alone for a number of years. In the late twenties he had taken over the local militia — what was left of the regiment after it disbanded in 1919, saying that there would be another world war. He managed to be laughed at by everyone. He kept trying to recruit, and published small articles on European and German military readiness. He had his boys marching about town in 1937, and took them into the woods to learn how to cut pulp and climb trees, in places like Neguac and Tracadie. He did this for strength training for his soldiers; to strengthen their legs and upper bodies. All his boys cursed him privately, in the middle of those bog-fouled places.

Then war came. The boys became men. They went overseas. Men all about them were killed, but the core of those soldiers he had trained in Neguac and Tracadie, like Mr. Foley, went through D-Day and beyond, with few casualties. He was proud of this. He should be.

He was growing old even when I knew him; a tiny fellow with red lines in his face. His biggest love besides his vegetable garden was hockey. He loved baseball as well, and would travel about in the summer with a Dodgers' cap on, go to the baseball games in Chatham, and at times get down to Fenway.

"Baseball has my respect," he said. "I love it. The Chatham Ironmen are a great baseball team. And Loggieville is wonderful in softball. It is a game that has the smell of soil — and is alive and wonderful."

"I see," I said.

"Hockey has the smell of darkness, sweat, and ice — fire and ice," he said. "That is eternal."

His wife had died years before. He read military books and, like Montgomery, loved to instruct young men on what to do and how to act. But only if they came to him. He was trying to take Michael under his wing, but Michael had already learned to fly.

Now that the way of the world had changed, the war long over, the way the world viewed him had changed. Though he had not. He lived a Spartan existence, which meant during the summer inviting us into his house for vegetables out of his garden. I did this once a summer for six years.

I'll let you in on a secret. The vegetables in his garden were weeds. He ate weeds, and packed weeds away in his freezer for the winter.

Not a potato, turnip or cabbage grew in his garden. Just weeds. And he would invite us over at the end of August every summer, for a big bowl of weeds. Tobias would sit at the table, with a napkin tucked under his chin, shaking his head. It was as if the good Lord had played a number of tricks upon him — eating worms, and now, a bowlful of weeds.

"This is a new variety of creeping scalia," he would say. "It grows better in an arid climate than here — but is still tasty."

He would always give us some to take home. Pots of weeds. Tobias would take his weeds and head down over the bank, go into the house and set them on the table. Worse. For, as I say, it always gets worse. Bert always thought the old Colonel was making fun of her poverty, giving them five pounds of weeds. "He's one damn big-feeling man now, ain't he?"

The Colonel thought the greatest goalie who ever lived was Jacques Plante. He felt Plante knew everything — and this is what you needed to know — everything. And the Colonel was a stickler for knowing everything. He believed the greatest player in the last twenty years was a toss up between Richard or Howe. But they weren't Howie Morenz.

He thought hockey had gone to the dogs when they put in a centre line, but I knew little about this, or why he was upset about it. If there was no centre line we would have much faster games, he declared and be able to move the puck much better. And we would have to learn to move the puck. The terrible truth he told us, and it was instilled like dry snow on our souls. Instilled forever and ever.

He had witnessed it at Squaw Valley, the winter before when the Americans beat Canada 1–0 after being outshot perhaps 45–11, and won the Gold Medal. As he spoke he would sit in the kitchen chair puffing on his pipe and watching us eat our weeds.

"When we lose they are the first to notice it — when we win, they simply shrug — but we will be winning less and less if we don't fund our own league. The whole world is out to beat us and take our game. You can't say it any differently than that. You cannot be polite about it. Our best players are tied up in the States and we travel this year, to play in Europe. If we get beaten we will be laughed at — if we win, they will call us barbarians. There is no justice so we should only rely on ourselves."

He was the first to tell me about the European rinks being bigger than ours. He was the first to tell us that when expansion came it would go to the south. Even as far away as Florida. I didn't — couldn't believe this. And to me he had coined the phrase: "Hockey is life."

So, he said, as he puffed on his pipe, "If it goes south — which it will — we will sooner or later be left out of the decisions that matter in hockey."

It was sad to hear this from him. It might be all right to go toe to toe with my uncle and my cousin, but to go toe to toe with a man who knew more about the sport than I ever would, who loved his country, and yet still felt his country was damned as far as their national sport went, was another matter. It was sadder because I believed him.

He realized before anyone else realized it that no matter

if we had bragging rights in the NHL — it was a moot point to those, who never knew who we were, and moot also in Europe where they were beating our teams for the World Championships.

I couldn't disagree with him. Especially when he was feeding me a nice bowl of weeds.

By January of 1961 the old Colonel was listening to his radio. Of course he had been for years. The idea that the Americans had won the Olympics in 1960, rankled him. The Americans for God's sake.

The Americans were laughing at us, "laughing up their holes" was the expression we used on starry winter nights here. The Russians too, and we still did not have anything approaching a national team. We had teams from small towns going over to play for the World Championship. And it was back in 1960–61 I was first becoming aware of the disaster of it. I loved them, but it was getting more and more evident that they could no longer keep up. I was also beginning to hear the name which would become synonymous with every foul trick perpetrated against Canada by the Europeans for the next ten years — Bunny Ahearne, the persistent, diabolical, president of the IIHL. When Brendan Behan the Irish writer mentioned that Canada should stick to its league, ice hockey, we should have taken his advice. What Mr. Behan wouldn't have been aware of, is that an Irishman named Ahearne was trying to keep us from this as much as he could.

And now, in 1961, we were sending another team called the TRAIL SMOKE EATERS.

I can only tell you what I remember about them from my vantage point on the Miramichi. I had heard about them. And in my mind they were dark forms moving across sections of large unfriendly, unpainted ice, far away in another world fighting for us, and ready to be dismissed by many of us at any given moment. And I felt sad and apprehensive. I don't know whether I felt sad and apprehensive for them, for me, or for Canada. Perhaps it was for us all. And this apprchensiveness, or the memory of it, has never left me. I remember when they lost their first exhibition game against the Swedes, after travelling for days to get there.

Trail hadn't won the Allen Cup and were not the first to be asked. Chatham, Ontario, did and was, as Mr. Scott Young reports in his book *War On Ice*. But because of finances they couldn't take up the challenge. And it was left to Trail. It was left to Trail — a place so far away from me, from my view of Canada, from where I was, it was strange that they were representing us. Except we both knew, that is the Miramichi and Trail, what hockey meant to us. We could still smell the hockey blades in the fall night air.

I sometimes like to think that our attitude has gotten better since the Trail Smoke Eaters. Yet I think our international hockey has been like this: we have stuck our head in the sand and refused to really examine what we are doing and why we are doing it in our attitude toward our sport. It happened just as the old Colonel said it would, just as the Second World War did.

For years, all during the terrible seventies and eighties, we thought we had to find a system to beat the Russians or the Czechs, or the Finns or Swedes, and we relied on defence. Can you imagine, thinking we needed a special system?

For Canada to rely largely on defence is similar to having Joe Frazier decide that the best way to beat Mohammed Ali is not to throw his left hook.

"A lapse in defence" or "a breakdown in our own end" was always what cost us this game or that and our national coach for a number of years was always there to tell us this, and to reassure us, that once our defence got better, or once we played our positions, and remembered what to do, we would raise our game to the level of the opposition.

I am almost positive the Russians and Czechs and Finns and Swedes loved to hear this. This has nothing to do with me not liking defence — I remember Paul Coffey stopping a two-on-one against the Soviets in 1984 just before Canada scored the winning goal.

I remember being amazed at our three players on the ice for seven — eight minutes in the eighth game against five rushing Soviets in 1972. In their rink with their referee; with *their* system. And I can also say that I don't think it was a defensive system that made these moments so great for Canada. It was the absence of a system.

The one thing a defensive system did for Canada in international hockey was inhibit what we could do instinctively. Taking the man, and hitting him. And actually shooting. A system relying on defence always made a nation who relied on intuition a nation of second guessers.

Besides, the one thing we tried to curtail in our defensive systems of the seventies and eighties, was the one thing Canadian defence has always relied upon — hitting. We were frightened of hitting, because of our reputations. So we played defensively many times by doing anything but hit.

Defensive play often worked. It made us lose by two goals instead of four. At a certain point it broke apart anyway. And it broke apart because no matter what kind of team we sent to Europe our gut instinct told us that this was not us. No matter what the philosophy behind the bench was. Yet for years we tried this.

And we tried this defensive system for more than just hockey *on* the ice. We tried this system for public relations in Europe and at home. We tried this so the newspapers would be nice to us.

"They played a nice — clean game, with good back-checking, and lost 4–2 — the one thing I can say is that they acquitted themselves like gentlemen. But don't the Russians just dazzle —"

The idea was that we couldn't beat them but we could stop them from beating us. Too badly. This was the philosophy, and it got us some bronze medals in international play. And made me sick at heart.

For everyone was on pins and needles all through the late seventies and eighties when this philosophy was at its high water mark. We were on pins and needles because we were told — as we had been told for years and years and years — to stay out of the penalty box.

With a defensive system, we might clear the puck a half a dozen times, but sooner or later we're going to get caught in our own end. Sooner or later my friend we are going to take a penalty for holding or tripping the man. And then what else are we going to take, when trying, shorthanded, to clear the man screening the goalie in front of our net? A cross-checking penalty. So we are two men in the box for 3:22.

If you have relied on defence and you have two men in the penalty box and you have the Russian sharpshooters buzzing about — that's the game right there. Because the one thing we did when we relied on defence is for some peculiar reason not rely *on offence*. Even on a breakaway we would seem to be unsure of ourselves.

Team Canada, of '72 fame, two men short was still dangerous because they never had the man behind the bench telling them not to be. And they knew, like the Trail Smoke Eaters, that the last thing fair, in Europe, or in Russia would be a penalty call.

I am not meaning to slight these National teams of the recent past. They worked their guts out playing against great Soviet teams. Only such a system caused them their second-guessing. I know they tried their damndest. But they were not only fighting the great Russians or Finns, they were fighting their natural instincts, to take the other team to task — take the body hard and push the puck forward.

And sooner or later their natural instincts would bubble over and they would upend someone, or deek with perfect balance, and find themselves in the box. The game was lost anyway. If you are so terrified of penalties, that you mention it to everyone who ever wrote a line for a paper, you are almost bound to get more of them than you deserve.

As long as we play at our best, we are going to get penalties. This will be as true in 1998, as it was in 1958. There are always horror stories about refereeing from players who played in Europe. The first eleven penalties called would go to Canada.

This idea that you can make hay by blasting Canada, has been around for years. No team ever complained about Canadian backchecking on sensitive virtue alone. Virtue has nothing to do with it.

And it was always there. It followed the Penticton Vees and the Trail Smoke Eaters — just small town Canadian boys going over to play for the world, when all of Canada, like the old Colonel by his radio, knew what was really at stake.

Part Three

EIGHT

I WOULD LIKE TO MENTION THIS: I heard a song once by an old black man, from the south. And I said to myself: that does sound familiar — those guitar riffs, that old refrain; ah, yes — I remembered it was sung by a white rockabilly boy that winter of 1961.

It was not made famous by this old blues man — this sad old blues singer from Mississippi; it was made famous by the be bop a loo bop rockabilly boy with the white complexion, who could introduce the song to mainstream America — package it in a comfortable way to the girls who would not swing their dresses so high, wiggle too, too much.

It was a great song. At first, I liked the rockabilly version. The old man's version seemed so strange — so *foreign* to me, that I did not accept it.

The record company wanted the old blues song that came from blood and sweat in that Mississippi delta. They wanted the guitar riffs, the lyrics. But they wanted it not so troubling, not so rough. They wanted to hide it away, and tuck it in. And they didn't want the black voice husking out into the microphone.

But yes, they could profit from it. They wanted the song. They did not feel they had to tell you where this song came from. They did not feel a need to tell you that it came out of a person's love of country and gift of life and tragedy when both have been taken away. They didn't want those young college girls and boys — who so desperately needed a song such as this — to know quite what it all was about.

And those record moguls knew that they didn't need people to know the song's history in order to sell the song. Nor did they consider that if people did not know the song's history they might never know the song well.

But, as I say, I listened to it. I listened to the rockabilly version of this song in 1961 when I was a child playing hockey in the street. It was the rockabilly version under the cold sky that everyone tapped their toes to. It was the version that everyone heard which to them represented all the authenticity and spontaneity they believed the song had to offer.

Years later I heard the black man from the delta singing, in his gravelly voice this same song, in a house on a dark and solitary back street in Saint John, NB.

The rockabilly version is still out there. But now, nothing about it is so remarkable. It is a version with a mask, a front. It is still in its own way, something you might dance to, buy, or send as a gift, as memorabilia of that long ago lost age.

But the song, written and sung by the black man from the delta, goes beyond all of this. It is *now*, just as it was *then*. It has not lost itself in nostalgia. It has not changed. It is not dated, because it comes as it was written, in sacrifice and courage and love.

Those who invent the world for us, do this often. They legitimize by delegitimizing. For so many songs, ideas, books, opinions, etc., are best sanitized just a bit for the broader marketplace. The place where the glossy edition comes out.

The world is invented for us. It is made palatable. The old black man did not understand this. Some of the greatest songs of all time were written by black men who got fifty bucks for them.

The honour supposedly came when they listened to the radio and heard the be bop a loo bop, party-pack version on some rockabilly show, from somewhere in Tennessee. They were never mentioned as the inventors of those wonderful songs. Their names never spilled out onto the airwaves.

What does this have to do with my hockey book? I don't know. It's just something I thought I'd mention.

Back then from 1961 through to 1967, when we walked out in the snow after school the long shadows of evening were against the slanted frozen buildings, and the hockey game in Europe was almost over. We would always try to catch just a bit of it. Running home — I remember running home — we would pick up the CBC broadcast from Europe, amid the static, and when it finally came in, the sound of whistles and jeers from the fans. Sometimes there would be interference, and silence for whole minutes.

Then it would break out again. The sickening sound of whistles and jeers. I can never think of a game in Europe where the jeers and whistles did not fulfil some prophetic sense of doom, no matter which of those years we happened to catch it.

"What are they whistling and jeering at?" Darren would ask.

"Shhh — we got — two more minutes."

"Ohhh — " Darren would answer. And he would look in the kind of startled way children have. Stafford would fumble with the dial, his pants drooping, the back of his shirt untucked.

"Shhh."

Out of the corner and now up along the boards — here come the Canadians — now Dewsbury — here, now just a minute here we go again, Dewsbury is called — another penalty to Canada and the Czechs are up 4–2.

I remember hearing something very much like this when I came home from school in 1959. That was the year Bellville was wearing the Canadian colours.

I remember sitting with Stafford and Darren, shaking just a little. Darren sat in a chair staring at the wall. Stafford stood near the radio, as if moving the dial one fraction of a millimetre would bring in a better score and a different announcement. But it never did. Sometimes I would lay down on the couch and put a pillow over my head, listening, rocking back and forth, and hoping that my rocking would drown out the drone of whistles, the static, the idea that time was passing and we were behind.

Far away in Europe on those cold, shadow-filled arenas Canadians were playing for us. No one here could help them.

I don't know now – you get the feeling that Canada might not be able to make this up – that missing that breakaway – might have demoralized them a little.

And again we would wait and listen. And then usually clearer than anything else, the long ago beeping buzzer that would end the game. Rushing home from school to hear these games we would never really know what period we were getting, and so Stafford would always say hopefully: "Well there is probably another period." Only to find out that they were signing off, and there suddenly was string quartet music of some sort.

There was, in those long ago dark afternoons of 1961 some terrible hypersensitivity in me.

I knew something was strange in how others viewed Canadians – I knew the old Colonel was right in this, but I didn't quite know how it was happening, only that it was. I did not quite know how to explain it. We were the best and yet it seemed, after Squaw Valley, after Bellville losing to the Czechs and after the 4–0 loss to the Swedish team by the Trail Smoke Eaters that something very fundamental in our nature was missing.

We were cocky hockey players, but we were indentured. As I sat there in that office I was flooded with memoried pain of my uncle and his son, coming to our house, and telling us about how great the Russians were, and then having the audacity to go out and beat us.

The name Bunny Ahearne still drives me nuts. I did not know why then. How could I know? I only knew that everytime a decision about hockey was made it was made (with the backing of hockey powers like Saudi Arabia) to the detriment of Canada. The Canadians knew this — Bunny Ahearne knew this. Everyone, in Canada who gave a fiddler's fart about hockey, no matter how blind they were, knew there was an unfair, intrinsic mean-spiritedness about the IIHL treatment of Canada — that would not stop until 1972.

But the secret Bunny Ahearne, Irishman, had when brokering deals that would freeze Canada in International hockey was to play upon the Canadian ego and the Russian self-interest in keeping Canada as far on the outside as possible.

We felt we were the best and the toughest and the most talented. What could unfairness do to us? Or mean-spiritedness? Ignore it and get on with the game. I'm sure that this was the posture Ahearne *hoped* for in his dealings with us.

Ahearne had a peculiar antipathy for our nation that came with smiles one day and angry arm-twisting the next. Why he made us a scapegoat was a particular strain of angry envy, mean-spiritedness — and that peculiar idea that he had to be fair to the *others*. The IIHL was also a money-making venture for his own travel agency, (*Net Worth,* Cruise, David and Griffiths, Alison: Penguin, 1992).

But it was also the idea that their game, the European game, the game of *ice hockey*, was more *moral* than the game of hockey.

Well I know our hockey could be rough, uncompromising in the corners, hard-driven, knock your head off. But it could not, our game of hockey, be mean-spirited. And this is what we faced from 1959 until Paul Henderson's goal somehow delivered us in 1972. It was not so much that Paul Henderson's goal won the series (in the Russian Sports Hall of Fame they never tell you who *won* that series — they only tell you that the Russians scored more goals overall) but that his goal somehow delivered us. It proved to all of my generation for once what we thought and felt and believed about our country was essentially true.

That the Russians, could be *mean-spirited* — that they could flood the penalty box with our players, not give us meals before the game, try to keep us awake all hours of the night on the *conviction* that the world would understand that their game and their life was more MORAL. But finally on the ice — on the ice — hockey was greater than ice hockey.

I think of those times, cramped boots and coats, dark, dark afternoons, when the Trail Smoke Eaters were our hope in Europe, on a forty thousand dollar budget.

Michael and Ginette over the bank together shovelling

the snow from the rink, and then the nets made, and suddenly great railway ties coming from somewhere, for the boards.

Tobias thought he had a father somewhere. Suddenly Tobias believed his father was somewhere in Napan — and he knew who he was, because one of his relatives told him. He was excited about this. And Michael told him not to be.

At this time too, Stafford began to rebel — he began to reduce his insulin intake, believing he could eat candy if he did. We had left his house, and had gone down over the bank to help with the railroad ties Michael had collected. It was a clear night in February, the stars were dazzling, and suddenly, there was a sound. It was Stafford and his brothers fighting.

"Get some sugar into him — get some sugar."

He kicked, screamed and roared, and threw Darren off him as if he was nothing at all. Out of Stafford's back pocket fell two pamphlets that he had sent away for. They lay in the snow as a symbol of Stafford's hopeless hope.

He had collected twelve labels from Corn Syrup for these pamphlets. And for those Corn Syrup labels he had received: *How to train for hockey* and *How to play better hockey*, written by Lloyd Percival in the 1940s and adopted by the Russian program in the fifties. And still around in 1961.

He carried those pamphlets about with him like the two tablets of The Ten Commandments. He would read them and reread them with his half-blind eyes. Each pamphlet had a place for your name: *property of* Stafford Foley, 609 King

George Highway, Newcastle, NB, Canada, North America, Western Hemisphere, Planet Earth.

The pamphlets lay in the snow and were almost washed under a drift until Darren, who had a bloody lip, saw them and picked them up. Then we went back up the hill together, through the drifts, in the frigid air.

The secret was, he had drunk the corn syrup, sitting in his basement hidden behind the furnace. After this episode, he walked in a daze many days. Sadly it became known by us that he still wet the bed. Often at night the lights would snap on, and he would be wandering the house, soaked to the skin. A smelly bucket of pee sat under his bed.

One day just after this he began to question me about my grandfather. My grandfather was a diabetic and had graciously volunteered to be one of Banting and Best's guinea pigs. He was one of the first diabetics to try insulin, and died of insulin related complications.

When I related this story to him Stafford turned to me and clutching my arm with his small brave hand said, "Thank your granddad for me," and smiled.

Like Michael he had already seen the depths and was at times tired, very tired of swimming.

I remember the path Michael took to get those railway ties down to his rink. In 1961 there was one squad car in the town police force, driven by Sergeant Hood, and there was the paddy wagon. The paddy wagon had a stickshift and shifting between second and third caused the whole engine to shiver and the truck to knock. We could tell when the paddy wagon was coming at least a half a mile before it arrived.

Michael would go out after dark wearing his leather gloves, his jean jacket, and, hauling a sled, would walk to the tracks where he would steal two replacement ties at a time and haul them down past the creamery. Once on the creamery lane he would swing to his left over a snowbank and cross the dark field. He was in Skytown territory now, and ran the risk of getting his ties stolen by the Griffin boys who had their rink just beyond Morrison Lane.

He wore no hat though it might be -15°F — he always believed that exercise would keep him warm.

He would cross Old King George Highway, and through the apple orchard to King George Highway. Once on his lane he was safe. He would haul the ties around to the back of his house and hide them. Then waiting an hour or so he would bring them down to his rink.

Michael's rink was beginning to look as fine and as accomplished as the Sinclair rink. And he knew this. We skated and played hockey on his rink now, with the bubbles of air trapped in the ice under the icy moonlight and a fire going. We all believed we had a great hand in it, but actually it was he and Ginette who had never given up on it.

Now they could not tell him he did not belong to a team. And no-one was going to tell him that he couldn't play the game. That was the right, and the legacy, of every Canadian child.

He never invited you into his house, and almost always tried to refuse to go into yours. He never spoke about owning anything. He didn't compete with the boy who showed him his new hockey pads and Tacklebury skates. He could never brag about his dad getting a car, or a truck. But once you were on the lane or street, or down at his rink you were on his territory and he knew he was on even ground.

There were a lot of tough boys in the neighbourhood, and he was as tough as any. I remember this now, again that in my small block of neighbourhood houses and garages I knew a cross-section of life that homogenized middle suburbia never has experienced.

Those times in the dark night air with his woollen sweater on, smelling of his house, flicking the pucks at us and smiling as he skated backwards, turning on a thin dime and breaking into strides that seemed to swallow the ice — at those times, the hurt wherever it came from, was all gone away, and he was free.

Where we had once lived seemed so little that day, in 1989, walking with Paul. Coming back to the town — everything seemed smaller, less important. The mill was now three times the size — and our river had lost its innocence. Where the gully once was, the new yuppiedom had built spectacular houses to overlook it, and no small boys and girls played on a rink. Now and then there was still the smell of smoke but it did not bite the sharp night air as it used to.

The house where Michael and Tobias lived had been torn down years before, and the lane near the creamery where Michael had dragged his railway ties looked very small and ordinary. The field too was gone.

My father's theatre had disappeared and was replaced by videos. The young generation — mine, was hurrying along to middle age. Our children were as much interested in baseball and soccer as anything.

Hockey had become a sport dominated by a new ideal. Hardly a child I knew back in my day would have been able to afford hockey now, the way its costs had skyrocketed.

All of this Paul and I talked about on the way to where we were going.

There were not as many fires in the winter either, in which people lost their lives, as there were in our town of grey wooden buildings when I was young.

The Sinclair Rink was gone also — it had been burned down by some boys in a hoot, and was replaced now by the Miramichi Civic Centre.

I thought back, to those foolish thoughts Stafford and I once entertained; that when hockey expanded it would expand to Newcastle — that we would have our own NHL team. (In the part of me that has never been able to grow up, I still think we could do this — that the Hartford Whalers do not deserve a team. Certain hopes you have as a child keep you one forever. That, to quote Robert Browning, is what a heaven is for.)

And looking down at the river it was as if I could see us all.

NINE

THE TEAM MICHAEL SHOULD have been on was doing well. They beat Bathurst 3–2, which was never supposed to happen. The little peewee they had brought up, Tony LeBlanc, who had scored against Boston, was scoring for them. He had scored on a breakaway against Bathurst with a minute and ten seconds left. He was no bigger than Stafford. Yet he could move about you as if you were standing cold; he slipped through checks all year long, and he came out of nowhere from behind the net, could always tuck the puck behind the goal tender, and then raise his stick with one hand as he glided into an embrace, his big Bantam A shirt down to his knees.

A dozen times in a game you thought he would be creamed, only to watch him slip through, and head towards the net. And the older boys seemed to be like big brothers to him.

I mentioned that they had brought Darren up from the Peewees as well and had put him on the wing. The team had jelled since its loss to Boston, and was waiting to go back to

Boston in the spring to exact a terrible revenge. Even Phillip Luff knew enough to pass the puck so others could score.

The rink was becoming filled again for the Bantam As. Suddenly there was the idea that the town had a team again — kids who were giving everything they had, wearing ancient hockey sweaters and mismatched socks.

In the house league that Stafford and I still played in, we too had spectators — small children who had figure skating before us, the few rink rats who were obligated to be there, the woman who ran the concession stand, and a few mothers and fathers. Also the coach, who was the coach of the Bantam All-Stars also, and who Stafford was a terrible suckup to. I suppose he knew I knew, and only wanted me to realize that he couldn't help it.

Now and then, playing his heart out he would be castigated by the mother of one of the other players for allowing the team to fall behind. "Are you blind?" Sharon would yell at him. Stafford would wipe his eyes, would look over, smile and keep on going.

"Ah get off the ice and go sit down — who are you — the coach's pet — hang around the coach — don't worry now boys you can just *waa — lk* in and score — *walllk* in and *sc-OORE*. *Idiot arse* is on the ice again. Ole Idiot Arse Piss the Bed is on the ice."

And so it spread, and Stafford was known, secretly as Piss the Bed and Idiot Arse. If you went over and told people he was a sleepwalking, fall-down diabetic with a maniacal desire to participate in events normal children around the country did, it might have made a difference. But he did not do this. Nor would he want anyone else to.

Of all the people who ever yelled and screamed at the coach or children, or bullied, I found mothers to be by far the worst. The most vicious. Every moment on the ice must have been agony for some children. And Stafford was one of those children. Those who made it with ease, like his brothers, or those who refused to let it destroy them like Michael would not have much idea what Stafford went through.

Sometimes we would stand there, as the play just carried on about us, nodding now and again to the other players as they skated by. Once or twice when Stafford touched the puck, usually having it hit his stick — he would yell out to the coach, his face gone mad with glee, "I touched the puck — I touched it."

"Ya, good — great," the coach would say. "Keep up the good work."

Worse, was when Stafford's sisters would arrive and yell out to us, "There's Rocket and Pocket — there's Rocket and Pocket."

And we would skate a few blades, like grilse moving out of their position, nodding toward the bleachers, then try to skate backwards to our lay again.

But there were a few things I learned from those days. One was the viciousness certain adults have toward those who do not measure up. You are most often ridiculed by lesser men.

We played from eight o'clock until about ten minutes to nine on Saturday morning; then the Bantams would take over and then the Juveniles. The later in the day it was, the older the teams got, the more serious the players looked, until just before three o'clock you had players skating about with five o'clock shadows.

One morning we were playing the first place house-league team – the Bruins. Stafford and I were at our blueline, watching the play develop up at the other end of the rink. It looked like we were going to score, but we didn't. The puck tricked out and one of the Bruins grabbed it. Emmett, who looked like a small pitbull.

Away he came towards us. And we stood there watching him. Quite politely we felt he would just *wisshh* by us. We would nod to him like we usually did. And that would be it. This had nothing to do with our not wanting to stop him. We wanted to stop him – we just weren't sure how.

But this morning as he came down the ice towards us, he noticed me as I stood on the blueline, and putting his head down made a quick turn to his left – right in Stafford's direction.

"Get out of the way," I yelled at Stafford. "Get out of the way."

Emmett did not see Stafford of course. Most people did not see Stafford. Nor did Stafford move. Perhaps he did not have time. Perhaps he just said the hell with it.

Everyone on both benches was yelling at him to get out

of the way. Our coach, their coach. Sharon. But Stafford was frozen.

At the very last second Emmett looked up. I saw Stafford close his eyes.

WAMP.

Stafford went about fifteen feet in the air, bent in at the stomach like a rag doll before he hit the ice, and then slid, round and round like a top, his head wagging one way and then the other. He had saved a goal. He was knocked out cold. That was perhaps the high crest mark of our friendship.

But the next Wednesday evening, something put a strain on Stafford's and my relationship. That was the day the puck touched my stick, was picked up by Earl McIntosh and Earl McIntosh flipped it into the net.

"I got an assist," I said. I could not believe my luck. I was on the score sheet, in the House league's scoring RACE.

The evening was quiet when we left the rink. Cars moved off as frozen and grinding as fingers down a chalkboard. I walked with my coat half-opened, and breathed the air, insensitive to the cold.

"It wasn't really an assist," Stafford whispered, when we got to George Street.

"What do you mean?"

"I mean I have seen many assists in my time, and that was about as phony an assist and everything like that — that I have ever seen."

"Don't care."

"Yes you do."

"Don't."

"Do."

"Don't."

"Do."

And we went our separate ways, at my street, not to speak again for awhile.

TEN

I REMEMBER HOW STAFFORD stuck to those tiny yellow hand-books written by Lloyd Percival. He tried to exercise every-day in the open air — which meant he left his bedroom window open and froze the upstairs out. Because this is what Lloyd told him to do.

There was a greyness to the snow, the earth itself. All winter long, lights from across our windswept river flicked out like beacons on faraway islands. For months there seemed to be nothing but small paths along the sidewalks, and snowbanks as high or higher than our houses.

And Stafford exercised in his small sleeveless T-shirt, star-ing into the dark. *Lloyd* had told him to do it. His stretches and his toe touching and his limbering up for the big game that never came.

He kept a progress chart on his wall, and did practice shooting outside at a tin can. Night after night just after sup-per he would go outside with his tin can and his hockey stick, and try to flick a puck and hit it, like the man in the movie *Liberty Valance*, a string of lights over his head, and half the lights burnt out. Stafford Foley's rink had disappeared by this time and was a trough of water and ruts covered with new, white snow.

He tried to jump over a broom handle. He practised stopping and starting quickly, but only in his rubber boots, and of course he tried to stickhandle and deek a board.

From my window I would often see him running about this board, like a squirrel in a cage. I never quite knew what it was he was doing.

I suppose he was a Lloyd Percival addict. He was the first person I remember who insisted his mother get wholewheat bread. His father would take a bite of it, spit it back on his plate and say, "What in Christ is this?"

He ate fruit and vegetables, and walked about with a chunk of cheese in his pocket. He almost never ate the cheese — he just had it in his pocket. He started a regimen of weightlifting. I have often considered the wounded as being the ones obligated to do this. By the end of March he was lifting 30 to 40 pounds.

At school he stayed away from me. During the whole time the Trail Smoke Eaters were over in Europe he never spoke about hockey to me. I think half of the reason Stafford stayed away from me is because I was so fanatical about Trail. I was a psychological menace to everyone in Canada when Canada was playing international hockey.

All during this time, my relatives in Boston made no calls, and we heard nothing from them. We were supposed to go down to Boston at the end of March — of course I was going as a tagalong; and I knew that if Trail did not win the World Championship, I would have nothing to say. In fact, I would want to say nothing. I wouldn't even want to go.

The Colonel told me that no one had given Trail much of a chance but that he thought they could win, and then he put, "At least the silver." Silver was no good, and never has been any good for Canada — there is not a team who ever played for Canada who has won a silver and actually wanted it. This is one thing about hockey. No Canadian ever felt great about a silver medal. It shows you where the game stands in our psyche.

When Trail was overseas, I began to get the first solid impressions of our opposition. I still thought of them on outside arenas far away, but I was essentially beginning to differentiate one team from the other. To know them as chunks of their country's personalities.

For instance, no matter how much I admired Mats Naslun later on, I disrespected the Swedes then, and now, and forever. I felt they were bogus world champions whenever they claimed to be. I have always felt that at our best the Swedes would never be a match for us.

I feared, hated, respected and admired the Russians.

I didn't feel it then, but over the years I felt that they were the one other country which could make a legitimate claim to the World Championship. That is often why, when in those contests in which some other country wins the World Championship or the Gold medal, it is more important to us how we fared against the Russians. I know the Russians feel that way about us.

"There is one team Canada has always had to watch — the back-door team — the Czechs," the Colonel told me in early March of 1961.

The Czechs I also knew. I liked them more than either the Swedes or the Russians. I didn't know them well, but I assumed at times that they *liked* us. The Swedes would never give us a wink. Definitely not the Russians, the Czechs might. At least I thought this way for a while.

Canada. Well God knows what I thought. Canada was always the team to beat at these affairs even when they weren't seeded number one. That is, every other team got *up* to play Canada.

Stafford decided that I was no longer his friend. He would come over to my side of the street and call for Garth instead of me. He would often leave when I showed up to play on Michael's rink.

I was no longer his friend because I had gotten an assist. I finally brought this up to him.

"Oh ho ho ho — you think that's what it is," he said. But he didn't elaborate. He was betting money on Detroit. Detroit was this and Detroit was that, and there was nothing anyone could say. He was a Lloyd Percival, Detroit-loving fool. I knew

Detroit would make the playoffs, but I was hoping for Montreal — who actually had the most points that year.

Everything was Lloyd Percival. The reason I didn't make the Peewee All-Star team was because I hadn't read Lloyd Percival. The reason he was now very strong and was going to make it, was because of Lloyd.

One night I went out alone — using my hockey stick as a spear more than as a stick, playing Eskimo and throwing the stick at the huge snow bears the grader had made, walking towards the river.

On the rink was one person. Stafford. The wind was blowing across the river and cut right through my coat. It lashed at my face and my eyes watered. It was probably −30°F. It seemed to be even colder on the windswept river. Far across the ice, lights from the other shore twinkled numbly and as remote as stars. Far away too, there were the lights of the other towns. We seemed to be the only inhabitants of the planet.

Stafford had set up his Lloyd Percival obstacle course and was going through the motions. But it was as if his heart was no longer in it. Tin cans that he skated around at so many feet apart. He was so light, that the wind blew him backwards when he stopped to take a breath and wipe his eyes.

And then he went over to the corner and took off his skates. He was in terrible pain. I sometimes forget that he was often in pain. He had a hard time lifting his feet into his boots, and when he did, he hobbled up the path towards me. I simply stayed where I was and he walked right by.

I then went down to the river and stepped onto the ice. Michael had made a fine rink, with backboards and a perimeter of railway ties. It was the finest rink Michael would ever make, with gill mesh nets frozen into the ice. And it would be his last. But I tell you being on it all alone at 9:30 at night gave you the strangest feeling. It was as if I was as far away from the world as any child who had ever existed.

I looked at the Graves Beans cans Stafford had set up, which were now being scattered by the wind, making soft clinking sounds against the frozen pods of snow, and felt suddenly as lonely as hell.

In March of 1961, the news came out of Europe – the Czechs had beaten the Russians, and were playing the Canadians. The Colonel was right. The Czechs were the back-door team. No-one paid much attention to them – but they had beaten Bellville two years before and now they had beaten the Russians.

I was on my way to the dentist when I heard. I was happy the Russians lost. I'm always happy when the Russians lose.

A thaw had come and the sidewalk in front of me was filled with a bloated fog, while water dripped from the buildings. I thought that if the Czechs had beaten the Russians that was good, only if we beat both the Russians and the Czechs.

We tied the Czechs a few days later, on an open-air rink, and so had to beat the Russians by two goals or the Czechs would win the Gold.

How many tournaments have the Canadians been in where their backs are not against the wall?

Some of our moments on the ice are essentially as heroic as our moment at Dieppe. Certainly one must not take this as being disrespectful. It is a part of our national character I am talking about.

Our backs were against the wall in the game against Russia in 1961 just as our backs were against the wall when we were 1–3–1 in Moscow in September of 1972.

My dentist back in March of 1961 was a tiny drunken little dentist. He was so drunk the day we tied the Czechs that he forgot to freeze my teeth, and went to the legion for a drink. "I'll be back when your teeth freeze," he said.

Then he came back, after an hour or so, and began to drill into the back tooth. It struck me as not being that painful, and I thought I might get away with it, when all of a sudden "Yoooulwl," and I jumped straight up out of my seat.

That is the only thing I remember about the day we tied the Czechs. For years and years the only thing I was to remember about the Trail Smoke Eaters is that I spent half that month in a dentist chair.

He also lay a bet with me that the Trail Smoke Eaters would not win. He may have done this just as a joke or he may have actually believed it. It was not all that difficult a thing to believe. They had a game against the Soviets coming up, where they had to beat them by two goals. The bet was 50 cents — my weekly allowance.

My dentist was working on one tooth. The filling kept falling out. I would wake up in the middle of the night howling in pain. And in the late foggy afternoon I would make my way back downtown. All the snow, all the dirt, fog and icicles in the town seemed to know my tooth was sore.

Years later when I was to a dentist in Saint John, he looked at an ancient filling I had received and said, "I haven't seen a filling done like that since I went to dental school with old such and such."

"That's him," I said.

"He was very bright — a wonderful human being — used to drink a little — was a devoted socialist, loved children."

"I never knew he drank," I said.

"He was a wonderful hockey player — college player — all the girls loved him."

"He never told me," I said.

"He lost his wife and child in a fire — that caused a lot of grief in his life."

I never thought when I was so young of adults once having been young, of having hopes dashed, children lost, their lives tragic.

It snowed again, and began to snow hard, and kept it up for days. For days, Michael went down to the rink and shovelled it off, only for it to be covered again that night. Michael was hoping to have a big game, with someone.

I had told my relatives from Boston that the reason we were

such great hockey players — people like *me* — was because of being born in the ice-ridden and snow-driven North. Of never minding either ice or snow or wind. Of not caring if it drifted for days. Of being unmoved by temperatures of −60°F. Of laughing at it all.

My uncle had been to Alaska to sell Cotts. He told me that Alaska was the coldest place on earth. He told me that whenever they wanted to sing about a cold climate, they didn't sing about Canada — they sang about Alaska. Whenever they wanted to talk about a gold rush — they talked about Alaska. Whenever they wanted to show you a polar bear in a movie it was almost always an Alaskan polar bear. Very few Canadian polar bears got their snout into a movie, he told me.

"North — to Alaska — we're goin' North — the rush is on — way up NORTH — Way UP NORTH," he began to sing.

"Canada is bigger than Alaska," I said sheepishly.

"Alaska," my uncle said, puffing on a cigar, "is even bigger than *Texas*."

"NO," my father said, because he was surprised, "Is IT?"

"'Fraid so," my uncle said, "'FRAIDD SOOO."

My father looked at me, and I said nothing.

Not only had they beaten us at Squaw Valley, we were not even the coldest country. And if we were the coldest country we wouldn't be able to brag about it, only apologize for it.

March 12, 1961, about one o'clock in the afternoon Maritime time.

Canada was penalized against Russia at the 40-second mark. Canada was penalized again at about the three-minute mark.

No one listening to that broadcast would have realized that not only were they listening to history — that this would be the last time a Canadian amateur team from the boonies, from the dark, smoky backwoods of Canada, would go over and win a World Championship, but that they were witnesses to the profound psychology of Canada and Canadian teams who personified this.

Canada would have to hold off a Russian power play for about five minutes at the very start of the game. When entire games could be decided. Canada managed, with Russians all about their net, to hold them off.

Canada scored at about the ten-minute mark.

Canada scored twice more in the second period.

Canada scored twice more in the third. The Soviets scored once.

And that was the game — and the World, and the Czechs were crying. The Canadians too.

For hockey was always more than a game, a scrap of ice, a puck shot at a net. *The Trail Smoke Eaters.* No one had given them much of a chance.

I went outside and it was starting to snow gently. A puff of white smoke came from the creamery far off. A train was moving slowly, the day was darkening. Some kids playing hockey shouted out to me as I walked.

I did not know I would be in my 40s before the World Championship became ours again.

I did not know that the most exciting hockey ever played since the game came into being, was still over eleven years away.

Part Four

ELEVEN

THE TRAIL SMOKE EATERS were mentioned in the House of Commons. In those days Ottawa seemed as far away from me as Prague.

Hockey was mentioned in the House of Commons again in '72. It was mentioned in 1987 when our World Juniors were involved in the fight with the Russians.

However the most famous occasion it was mentioned in our House of Commons – in recent times – was when Gretzky was going to L.A.

That Mr. Gretzky's going to L.A. was mentioned in the House of Commons was picked up by American television. It was also big news in the Soviet Union. The idea that Canadians were concerned that a great Canadian hockey player was going to play in the States was newsworthy.

"Why should he go there if he is a Canadian?" one Russian hockey fan asked on a CBC news program.

Such interest was a very strange thing to me. It was as if

we suddenly decided to stop a grain of sand in an hourglass. It was a great grain to try to stop — perhaps the greatest. But my God — Orr, Hull, Howe, Savard, Izerman, Coffey, Messier — one can conceivably go on for hours.

To mention Gretzky was, in fact, an insult to Canadians. Nothing more. For if no one thought about the great Bobby Orr going to Boston, no one thought of Canadian hockey as heritage we were content to piss away.

Christ, who was the greater player — Orr or Gretzky?

But it also allowed a misconception to be reinforced — that we, in Canada, were actually concerned about our hockey players, and that Gretzky was somehow the exception rather than the rule. That our players played for Edmonton — and *their* players played for L.A.

Perhaps it should have been mentioned in the House of Commons, but it goes to show that sometimes in Canada, even when you win, you are bound to lose.

It was in mid-March of 1961 when Stafford gave up on Lloyd Percival. I remember passing him one night as he stood in a phone booth, talking, with his big, brown earmuffs sideways on his head. He turned and looked my way briefly and turned back. The sky was cold, the long King George Highway stretched forever. I was walking down to the store.

I had already been to the curling club four or five times and I had asked him to come with me. The curling club ice was pebbled; the stones looked too huge to lift. And I really thought I was not going to be able to curl either — that I was doomed. I couldn't follow the scoreboard. Besides this, it was a game that people older than my father played.

"Yes, yes — I remember your grandmother playing here a few years ago," a man said to me.

"My grandmother — good, good."

"And there's old Mr. Bell who plays with one leg. So if you have a bad leg you should be able to fit right in here — we'll fix you up with a sport."

"Fine. Great," I said.

I learned later on that, as with hockey, curling was our game, and we *hated* when we were beaten at it. I learned also that the same things about hockey applied to curling.

1. That it was part of our national consciousness and we couldn't separate ourselves from it.

2. The Europeans and now and again the Americans, would become much better.

3. That we were abundantly generous with our time and our coaches and our clinics, to help other nations.

4. As long as we were the very best, we would never have it as an Olympic game. Only when the Europeans felt that they could match us in prestige would they allow us, and therefore themselves, this.

5. Once again, as in Bunny Ahearne's day, countries such as Saudi Arabia, or Kuwait, would get a vote on Canadian sport.

Curling was so closely linked to hockey in the winter in small towns that they became almost interchangeable. In our town, as in most, the rinks are next door to one another. But at this point in life Stafford did not think much about curling.

Often at nine at night his father would be driving about the neighbourhood looking for him. He began to hang about with a guy named Jimmy J. Jimmy J. was nineteen then. I think he still hangs about with boys and girls about puberty age.

Jimmy J. was married at this time. He had a step-son of seven or eight who he used to hang about with. His wife was a hair dresser. At this point in his life he drove a milk truck. He always had a dozen kids of puberty age or younger in his milk truck driving them somewhere. His marriage did not last that long — about a year.

He was very tall and thin, with cowboy boots, and a sandy coloured brushcut. Anything kids were interested in, he would get — he had his own go-cart.

I remember Stafford and Jimmy J. sitting in the milk truck. Jimmy J. had a cigarette behind each ear and one in his mouth. He had a rabbit paw on his keys. Stafford had a cigarette in his mouth too.

I saw them in at White's Pharmacy as I walked home. "Trail won," I said to Stafford, "Trail won — we won, we won — TRAIL — we won."

Stafford looked at me as if he were bored, blinked and said nothing. He held a cigarette in his left hand, down near the stickshift so I wouldn't see it. I was angered by this.

Jimmy J. laughed and Stafford too, half-heartedly. But the idea why they were laughing only became evident when I got home and looked into the mirror. There was my mouth, all wobbly and twisted sideways. I hated the dentist at that moment, even though I had won 50 cents.

It was the only time Stafford ever laughed at me. Yet for a time everything was Jimmy J. The Foley kids had a huge fort built near their rink — with windows and small tunnels leading under the snow towards the house. One night as I walked by I saw Jimmy J.'s head poking out a window.

"Go way, go way," he said to me, and he ducked his head back in, and then out another window, and laughed.

The accepted idea — the idea that made Jimmy J.'s mental state agreeable was that he liked children. And there was nothing wrong with this. The years have been very hard on this idea. For a man who likes children now — as I do — treads dangerous waters. People have seen too much or heard too much or worried too much.

But back then, with his head poking out of a snow fort he was simply Jimmy J. And everyone knew him.

When we played hockey, Stafford would play if Jimmy J. did. And at times he played with us, he and his step-son. While his new wife started to go out with *friends*.

One night at the rink, I remember him bowling us over, a huge grin on his face, slashing everyone in his way. The idea of him being stronger or bigger than us did not give him any moral responsibility towards us. However Jimmy J. was unconscious of any of this. He had a huge grin, a new hockey stick and he said his favourite team was Detroit. He would arrive in his milk truck. He considered himself a company man.

Stafford was swearing, smoking and wearing his shoulder pads when they went anywhere; so he would look like "a pretty big chunk of a young lad."

Jimmy J. also talked about doing people in. Although I also felt even then that he was as scared as a rabbit, he had this idea that he was the bad lad on the block.

He said that if anyone did anything to him, he would put his hand into that man's chest and haul the still-beating heart out, and hold it up in front of the man's astonished eyes.

People my age were often as not very polite to him. They went to Foley's Tire Garage at night. In the old front office with its old desk, its brochures for lubricants and oil. The wind would howl and Jimmy J. would sit about and take stock of affairs.

He would sit at Stafford's father's desk and Stafford would be run off his feet doing errands for him.

"Get me a bag a those there chips Staffy," he would say. Or, "What I'd really like right now is a slurp of pop."

The pop was in one of those old machines that looked like an assembly line of pop. You fed one bottle along to a latch that would lift up if you put a dime in.

Jimmy J. would rarely pay a dime. He would tell Stafford to pay from his father's register. The whole thing about Jimmy J. was his feeling that he would: "Do it for you, Staffy."

And Stafford would break into the register and give him the dime. Then he would stand there smiling as Jimmy J. downed the bottle of Coke in one drink.

Stafford was all Jimmy J., just as he had been all Lloyd Percival. I didn't get to go with the Bantam As when they went to Bathurst to play the Saturday after Trail won the World. But Stafford and Jimmy J. hitchhiked. Stafford tried to dress like Jimmy J., walk and talk like Jimmy J.

Until something happened that was just as strange.

Tobias thought he had a father. It was just an idea which no one minded. His father was going to do this and his father was going to do that. His father lived in a big house and was going to invite him there. If his father came home, you would see something. If you saw his father, you'd know.

He would sit on the edge of Stafford's bed and talk about his father. His father had to go away, but he was going to come back. In the cold, dark room Stafford took his insulin shot and still checked his hockey report, and still listened to Tobias.

Stafford had no idea about Jimmy J. really. He told Tobias to go with him to the creamery one afternoon. They would see Jimmy J., and get a drive about in the milk truck, and find Tobias' father. And up to the creamery they went. Ran really.

There was almost a visceral change in Jimmy J. He did not want Tobias in his milk truck. He didn't want him near. And if Tobias came by again, he would beat up Tobias. Stafford was his friend, and not Tobias. And Stafford should have known better.

But Stafford didn't know better. He only knew that Tobias was at their supper table five nights a week, that in actual fact there was something so mean about not protecting Tobias that it was unnatural.

Stafford simply smiled. He thought Jimmy J. was joking. But Jimmy J. took the hose used to wash the milk from the cement floor and hosed down Tobias, with a force that threw him back onto the ground.

"There," he said, "that'll teach ya. Go find your father now ya little bastard. I'm not looking for yer father I'll tell ya — right Staffy — I'm not looking for *his* father."

Tobias in the cold darkening March air, with the smell of sulphur from the mill so far away, turned and began to walk home, water dripping from every inch of him.

"That'll teach him," Jimmy J. said. "That'll teach him."

Stafford turned and caught up with Tobias. When they got to the bottom of the creamery lane they heard the milk truck behind them, with the door banging opened and closed.

"Get in this truck Stafford — get in this truck."

But Stafford did not get into the truck. He took Tobias to his house, and using towels from the bathroom tried to dry the boy off. Later that night he heard the creamery truck going back and forth on his lane.

After this there was a campaign waged for Stafford by Jimmy J. He would come along and ask him to get into the truck.

"No, I won't get into the truck."

"Well then, you are no longer my *friend*."

Stafford wouldn't answer.

"No longer my *friend* – no longer my *friend*."

Still Stafford would not answer.

Jimmy J. would go about the block. One day he picked up Garth and drove him about Stafford's house a dozen times, playing music from his radio, talking as loudly as he could every time he passed Stafford.

He tried to buy Stafford a hockey stick but Stafford said he had his own hockey stick. Then he began to tell secrets about Stafford. He telephoned his mother and said that Stafford liked *girls* and that Stafford smoked cigarettes. He also told us that Stafford had written a poem to Gordie Howe.

> *Gordie Howe Wow oh Wow*
> *When you come along the boards*
> *Everyone knows you scores*
> *Your greatness has just begun*
> *You'll lead us to the Cup in 61.*

After every assault upon him Jimmy J. would come back and talk to him. He would say, "Okay, are we friends now – I won't waste my time if you are not going to be my friend – friends for life or what?"

But Stafford did not want to be his friend. He played hockey with us again, and decided to improve his own backyard rink so he wouldn't have to walk down Green Street Extension and by chance meet Jimmy J.

After school he would go out and push his father's huge roller across his backyard. He wanted to relevel and flood the rink again.

One night Jimmy J. stood on the other side of the street, watching. "*Tits on a Bull*," Jimmy J. yelled. "*Useless as tits on a bull — DIA-BET-IC*," Jimmy J. yelled. "*DIABETIC*."

Stafford pushed his heavy cumbersome roller, as Jimmy J. stood on his tiptoes yelling and screaming at him. "*Insulin bag — insulin bag*."

But Stafford did not respond.

Now and then as Jimmy J. yelled, Stafford would stop to inspect a dip or a slant, go into the house and come out with a bucket of water to slosh it over his rink.

"*You'll have no rink like that — tits on a bull — ha ha ha — tits on a bull*."

Stafford would get on his knees and pat a part of the rink down, filling the holes with snow.

"*Are you my friend or what — are you my friend or what!*"

Stafford went into the house at dark and Jimmy J. loitered about the street for awhile and then made his way home.

The next night he was standing on the street watching the door, and waiting for Stafford to come out, when Michael came along. "Leave Stafford and my brother alone — ya nutbar."

Jimmy J. picked up a chip of wood and put it on his shoulder and walked back and forth in front of Michael. "Knock this chip off," Jimmy J. said.

Michael looked at him, came up with an uppercut and knocked him on his ass. The chip went flying.

Jimmy J. did not come back.

Years later I saw him, grey-haired and stooped, driving five or six kids about, all of them singing, listening to the top ten on the car radio.

TWELVE

I DON'T HAVE ANY copies of the Saturday *Star Weekly*, but for years it was the staple of homey Canadian living, with articles on everything from cooking to beaver dams.

It had an Ottawa or Toronto feel. That being said, it rested in various places in many shacks and shanties, and many houses too, across the country. I've seen it used to wrap salmon that my uncle brought down to us in the dark night. I've seen it in outhouses, and on the back shelf in garages. It was used to insulate porches, behind drywall, and it fluttered in the sleepy breezes on our car seats in July. It placed itself usually within the safe pedestrian bounds of common opinion, and rested upon its laurels as being the magazine that informed us in a never too dangerous way, about ourselves.

It showed the fashions. Had the glossy pictures.

Michael was subcontracted to deliver the *Star Weekly* on Saturday. He would pick the paper up from Darren in the morning and do the back road, Skytown and along the tracks.

This would earn him, maybe 50 cents, maybe a dollar. Darren would do King George Highway, down to Dunn's barber shop. Michael had the longer route.

There was a reason for this subcontract on Saturday. Darren did not consider himself welcome anywhere near Skytown — not since the Christmas of 1960. That was when he gave one of the Griffin kids a black eye in a fight — by hitting him in the face with a rock in his hand.

I think Michael did the route every Saturday for about eight weeks. Paper boys have a large turnover. Who can blame them? Everything Michael did back then to earn money was, in actual fact, child labour. To have to share two cents on a paper, on a freezing cold Saturday in February was pretty much like delivering the mail for free.

To do it with the sense of gratitude Michael had, or a sense of wonder that Tobias had, that his big brother had a job, seems almost farcical now. But other jobs were just as stingy. The money kids earned was almost always negligible back then.

Once down past the creamery lane he was in unfamiliar territory — in foreign land. The farther down the road he went, the farther he would have to go to come back.

There was also the idea implicit in all of this of the *attitude* of the Skytowners. Friendly could become unfriendly real quick. The neighbourhood rink you passed on your way down could turn into a cauldron of recruits on your way up.

Ganging up on someone was always considered cowardly. Yet there was a certain reasoning, where the idea of ganging up on a person was not considered low or mean-spirited. If you were in someone else's neighbourhood, if injury or insult was remembered, you were fair game.

Of course most of the time under those low winter skies this was benign, and no one bothered you. But there were fierce flare-ups into wars where twenty kids charged twenty kids with hockey sticks. Or when games on the neighbourhood rinks ended in a kind of pitched battle.

This particular incident didn't start on a March Saturday in 1961 — it started near Christmas of 1960. Everyone was playing hockey, and we had all wandered down to Griffin's rink to play. The Griffin boys began to tease the much-tormented Garth, and steal his rubber boot. This happened because of Garth's belief in Santa Claus. Nor did he know what to do except to break down crying. And this made everyone on the Griffin side of the rink howl and laugh.

Lorrie Griffin grabbed the boot, put it on his stick and began to run about the rink with it. It was a great victory for the Griffins.

I think that the worst thing Lorrie did that afternoon was not to steal the boot or refuse to give the boot back while Garth was chasing him about, slipping on his brown, well-tied, immaculately groomed, neat and clean shoe, but that he stood in the centre of the rink and began to wiggle.

No one can stand a victorious wiggler.

Garth was not the most popular boy in our group — but he did have the right to freedom of belief in Santa. I don't think Darren said, "I may disagree with what you say, but I will defend to the death your right to say it." Or express it in quite those terms. I think he said, "Okay then — I'll get a rock."

People sometimes forget that "defending to the death" might mean putting someone else to death. Darren rushed over, hit the wiggler in the eye with his fist. All of this lasted about a minute.

Garth grabbed his boot, and we all trudged over the snowbank and down the path, with chunks of ice and stones flailing about us.

They knew Michael was trudging his way into their territory each Saturday. But they needed some kind of a plan. A kind of attack from the rear. A kind of worry on Michael's part. A kind of — Tobias. They needed a Tobias. The weak link. The Achilles heel of Michael.

But they didn't know this is what they needed until they saw Tobias dawdling behind Michael one Saturday. He kept getting farther behind, as Michael rushed door to door to get the paper delivered. Finally Tobias had fallen back and was out of sight.

Michael went back to get him. He was leaning by a pole, looking up and down the street. "You wait here — right by this pole — and don't move — I'll be back for you," Michael said.

Michael turned, and then turning back gave Tobias a five-cent piece. "This is for yer help."

Michael never intended to go home that way. And he had not forgotten why. No one was going to bother him while he was delivering the *Star Weekly*. They were only going to show their heads afterwards.

Today he had to go back. For Tobias. By the pole. Around the corner.

He saw the Griffins at their rink.

The Griffin rink was far smoother on one side than the other, and it sloped high at the left corner so that the ball or, at times, the puck was always taking off and being lost. The Griffins had given Michael the idea of using those railway ties, which were lying about the tracks. But it was Michael who had managed to get them before the Griffins.

The Griffin rink was hidden from the road, so you could only see the tops of the kid's hats as you walked by, and now and then the grey ball hitting the top of an old aluminum shed and bouncing off into the shrubs.

You knew Lorrie Griffin by the long, green tassel on his cap, and you knew David Griffin by the yellow knob, like an eraser, over the butt of his stick.

Michael saw that stick with the yellow knob, the tasselled hat as he walked down. It was late in the day, and there was not a whisper from the hockey rink. Smoke peeled against the white sky. Everything was quiet. An old shattered goalie stick lay in the middle of the side lane, halfway up, deserted by someone.

And then the Griffins came out on the street. There may have been four or five of them.

As always, people who "double up on a friend," to use Albert Camus' expression, have a sense that they are not doing wrong because their purpose is more glorious than their method. Their action only fulfils this noble purpose.

The Griffins now thought they were very clever. They didn't think at all that they were being deceitful. Michael was cut off from Tobias, and Tobias was patiently waiting for him.

Michael had now stolen *their* railway ties. Michael had *kissed* one of the bucktoothed Griffin girls at the movie. Michael had *set up* Lorrie.

It would be nice to say that he went through them all. But he could not do that. They had their hockey sticks, and gloves, and he was standing with his empty paper-sack.

Lorrie began to wiggle, swing his stick.

Michael began to back away.

They began to run after him, and he led them on a wild goose chase. But first he ran up the side lane to pick up the broken hockey stick. He turned and swung it as they came. And this cooled their enthusiasm just a little.

So there was a Mexican stand-off without Mexicans. And here they were — Michael on one side, backing up slowly towards the edge of the woods. The five Griffins trying to surround him. They all got in a huddle and whispered — Lorrie saying, "You go that way and I'll come around by the shed, and you go over near the rink and come up over the —"

"Where?"

"Yous come up over the rink and come at him from that side and I'll —"

As they whispered this, Michael stood watching them, his coat opened, his chest half bare, his pug nose like a boxer's.

"Well are ya coming or what?" Michael said.

"We're comin — we're comin — just a minute or so — you wait."

"I'll wait."

As they whispered, a lone car passed them by. Perhaps every one of us has experienced this, as an adult. We turn a corner on a neighbourhood street and see a stand-off between children. It is where the universal rules of bravery and deceit are being played out, forever and ever, again and again.

This was what was happening as Garth and his parents drove by just then in their spotlessly kept Ford Mercury.

Garth had given up swearing for Lent — but Garth had never swore in his life. Garth looked out the window at them. "Those are the boys there mommie — those are *those* boys there."

His parents never knew that they sprayed snow over the shoes of the boy being sacrificed for their son's beliefs. The Griffins stood to the side to let the car pass. And that gave Michael his chance to disappear into the woods.

The Griffins took off after him. They ran through the snow and bushes as it was growing dark. They chased him as if he were a fox amid hounds. He could hear their shouts to one side of him or the other. You picture a Johnny Reb in the wilderness campaign of 1864 cut off from his troops, and trying to get back across the shattered lines — while the Yanks just keep coming.

Where was Michael going?

Well there was only one place he could go to. He was trying to make it down to the new King George Highway. At least there he would be closer to his own turf.

And he had to make sure he was far enough ahead of them that he could make his cut around them in the open field.

Night was coming on and there was the smell of metal and tar from the railway tracks.

The trouble was the Griffins were on his right and as soon as he stepped out they would see him. He stood up to his knees in the snow, leaning against an aspen, looking down over the silent side lane.

Every time he stopped walking, he could hear the crunching in the snow behind him. But now that had silenced too. Everything had become still — and the only example I can give is the one you feel when you are hunting deer. Everyone has hunted deer of course. Well then — think of the hour and a half between 4:10 and about 5:30. The woods suddenly, unmistakably and quite mysteriously *stop*. Its heart stills, no sound, no movement. There is an inevitable sadness to this hour. So still, so silent. It is the hour when the deer are beginning to move for the night. This then is what the woods were like. This is what it was like for Michael. He, too, would have to make a move.

Below him sat the Griffins' rink. And snow began to fall, with the air still sharp and smelling of metal. Suddenly Michael began. The snow crunched again, and he made a dash across the open field that led down to Hawkenbury's paddock. And of course the *hounds* were on him.

They came from both sides, and made a stab at getting him, throwing their hockey sticks in the air, that hurtled by him as he ran.

The lone mare in the paddock turned and the roar was on. Michael faced his adversaries with his broken stick, and picked up theirs to throw back at them. And turning again, making it past the mare, who snorted and thrust ahead, he jumped the fence and was gone.

He got home after dark, his paper-bag torn and his face bleeding. He sat on the cot for a moment catching his breath, and then he asked his old Gram where Tobias was.

"Ain't he with you?" she asked.

The room was dark. Across the lonely river the snow fell.

Michael went back out. He walked past the Foleys' and turned again towards Skytown, past the old Shell garage and Hawkenbury's friendless barn.

Tobias was leaning against the pole, sound asleep, waiting for his brother. The five cents he clutched in his small hand, like a pint of gold.

THIRTEEN

I HAVE TRAVELLED THE WORLD, after a fashion. I have looked for hockey scores amid the pictures of football heroes in *U.S.A. Today*, have read the thoughts on hockey by *Sports Illustrated*, and have watched hockey players in England do their skating sprints, from blueline to centre line and back again.

In the universities where a certain love of sports is often suspect, I have listened to the love of basketball and baseball replace my love over the years. Where the idea of an American basketball dream team of 1992 sent Canadian professors into a state of ecstacy — those same professors who often did not want to hear my complaints about the failure to promote our own dream team in Hockey.

We did not have it. And for years we could not manage it, and now our players are part of the melting pot. So Darryl Sittler's son plays for Team U.S.A. Bobby Hull's son, Brett, is an American. The melting pot has stirred us in.

The training grounds have shifted. There is something

more collegiate about the players today — and those colleges are in the States. The state university programs have promoted their own hockey with a vengeance.

Most of the players I knew never got to university.

I travelled to Virginia and, at night listening to the sports broadcast, I hear, after the talk about football, baseball, basketball and tennis — I hear a Canadian voice, and I glance at the screen. Some youngster from way up in Canada who cannot give his dream away — holds onto it as you would a pint of gold, and has driven down in his second-hand car, with his hockey equipment in the back seat for a tryout, in this small unassuming city near the Blue Ridge Mountains.

"I'm just glad the coach has faith in me and is giving me a try." He talks about being on the injured list, with a torn ligament all last year. That he got waylaid, failed to make the grade in some IHL team — but now he feels better. He has been skating with the team. He is about 25, and you know that everyone has given up on him, except himself. And I think again of Phillip Luff. Or perhaps Sean O'Sullivan. I don't know.

There is always a place where Canadians go when they fail. It is to another place — somewhere. In Virginia maybe, or in the U.S. Midwest. I have seen them.

In 1977 they laced up their skates in an arena in Barcelona. My wife and I watched them on television in a bar in Denia.

The European clubs. The Scottish hockey league. For some the dreams refuse to go away.

They are damned — not unlike Sisyphus — to do what the gods have condemned them to. The boulder is heavy and like Sisyphus their only relief is, as Camus says, that their fate can be overcome by scorn. Scorn for all the tricks the world has played upon them.

The "What ifs?" might someday stop. Like they did finally for Phillip Luff and dozens of others. Somewhere in an arena in Europe, a friend of my youth, playing in a small league in Northern Italy, suddenly thinks that the "What ifs?" did not only pertain to himself. They pertained as well to all of those other children, hopeless in youth, who sometimes hung about the bakery for a piece of bread on those long ago winter days before they went to school. The "What ifs?" pertained to the Michaels as well.

And in a way, in perhaps the best way, the "What ifs?" can never end. For something you have lived for will die if they do.

Phillip Luff could not let them end. For their ending would destroy his father, and his father could not allow them to end, for their ending would make his son ordinary, like everyone else.

Phillip tried out for team after team to go to the World Championship, the Olympics. He was always the last one cut, or nearly the last one cut. Or perhaps someone else was called up, just after he had made the cut, and they had to let him go. The coach told him he was one of the best players he had seen in a long while. He would secretly hope that Bunny Ahearne blacklist any Canadian player who even sniffed a

National League bench, in order for him to have one more chance.

His father kept trying to figure things out, make contacts that were getting harder and harder to make. Until Phillip was playing somewhere in the Midwest, for two hundred dollars a week. And then he came home one day. Perhaps he can't even bring himself to lace up a pair of skates anymore or watch a Canada Cup.

I've known other people like that. For years a man I knew said he could not watch a game because he knew too much about it. Not about what happened on the ice, but all the slow-burning acts of small betrayals that happened off that ice. He too had given it his all. He too had been cut, somewhere by someone.

The skates hang on the nails inside porch doors and are slowly forgotten. The children remember hearing that their father was once considered a good player — even better than good, no — he was a marvellous player. He could side-step a check in full stride, dish it out or take it — had a shot like a bullet, and most people were wary to mix it up with him.

And then something, somewhere along the line happened. Perhaps there was just nowhere else to go.

But don't kid ourselves. Many of them went everywhere they could, did whatever they had to do with their dream. And somehow, even with doing all the right things, having the talent besides, some of them got left out of the lottery.

Like one of the players we watched in Barcelona. All of a

sudden there he was, back in 1977 on that February afternoon. He took the puck into his own end ragging it, and then turned, like a young shark, and moved, and with a flick, you saw power and grace, and wisdom. He passed one player and then another, and then not having a shot he turned and began to rag the puck again skating backwards into the corner drawing the defence to him, and then passing to the centre man in the slot — wham, in the net — Le But!

He gave me that moment in Spain. Where did he go? And what has hockey finally given to him?

I was in Spain with my wife and son in 1995. We spent the winter there and played hockey on our patio. We would walk the beaches to collect bamboo sticks — ones that had knots at the bottom shaped like the blades of hockey sticks.

I was a pretty good hockey player by Spanish standards. I was able to flick a ball with my wrist shot over the villa and into our neighbour's yard, until an old woman began to complain in German that I was hitting her windows. It felt like old times.

Sometimes in the afternoons Spanish kids, getting off the bus, would stop and watch us and we would dipsy-doodle for them, among the coloured stones and hedges and red blooming flowers, wind up for scintillating slapshots, try to speak like Danny Gallivan or Foster Hewitt out of the side of our mouths.

My five-year-old son was always Wayne "Grebsky." I was everyone else. One time a Spanish kid sneaked into our yard and picked up my bamboo stick and tried to hit the ball. He finally whacked it against our wall, threw down the stick as if it was some kind of forbidden magician's wand and ran away.

My son wore his Montreal Canadien sweater into town even at the height of the Spanish-Canadian turbot war. He was proud of that sweater, and we weren't going to tell him *not* to wear it.

One afternoon a young Spanish woman who we knew and travelled with, had her friend bring us a hockey stick from Switzerland, with TEAM CANADA written on it. Because of the turbot war she wanted to show us how she felt about us.

Sometimes in the bars or walking through the quiet mid-afternoon streets, I would meet my *country*. Someone would walk by wearing a San Jose Sharks' cap, or a Los Angeles Kings' sweater with number 99 on it, a Pittsburgh Penguin sweater with Number 66.

It was a strange feeling. I suppose those Spanish kids, wearing those caps and sweaters, would never understand my mixed feelings. They were wearing my country and I could never claim that they were. I suppose my son was beginning to realize this although I did try to hide these feelings. Certain feelings of betrayal, of loss.

In Spain I read about the *American* hockey strike. In European papers when they spoke about the NHL they never mentioned Canada. They showed pictures of Mr. Bettman in his dapper suits, striding along a hallway. They spoke of the game in terms of New York and L.A.

I am not ten anymore, Quebec is on the verge of sepa-rating and my country is no longer mine. In Spain for the first time, I was desperately, proudly Canadian and yet didn't know if I would have a country in a year or two.

My country had become a strange place to me — a place where they felt the need to make 60-second mini-heritage commercials for our television and our theatres. These mini-heritage commercials showed who we are — that we invented things claimed by others — basketball, Standard Time, the Superman Comic hero, who fought for justice and the American way. Someday they might promote our involve-ment in hockey this way as well.

Yet you remember, that in the splendid and dazzling snowstorms, lying on a couch, watching a game with your girlfriend, you could still tell, with one eye half closed and thinking of other things, all that was brilliant about a pass or a deke.

I was asked in Virginia four years ago why I did not leave my country, go to the States to write. "Your country is going to break up," a gentleman said, not unkindly. "Quebec is going to go — you people on the Atlantic seaboard will be left to hang and dry — why don't you come to the States?"

"Hockey," I said.

There was more sadness than juvenilia about that answer.

In Spain we went to the shops and fairs, watched kids playing soccer in the sandlots and on the beaches.

There were beggars on the streets and little shoeshine boys who cheered for Real Madrid, Valencia or *Barth — thelona*. One with his little shiny eyes, and torn jeans, who kept admonishing me for wearing sneakers ran about all night in the cold air.

He had all the indictments already sworn out against him. His caginess, his false friendliness — the pretence that he always had something to do *for* me or to offer me. The idea that he would be *there for* me. All of this *is* part of the emotional signals of the artful dodger — the boy or girl left out.

And I thought, seeing him, that perhaps poverty is better served in warm climates than in cold. Although I am not the one to say. I was never nearly as poor as this shoeshine boy, or Michael or Tobias. They *knew*. Their eyes told me the same things as this child. His shoeshine box was essentially the same as Michael's snow shovel, with its taped handle.

Thirty-four years and thousands of miles away from one another their dreams were dreamed for the same end. One was for soccer — and Real Madrid — the other was for Hockey and Toronto Maple Leafs. One had palm trees over his head and cobbled streets where he kicked a small soccer ball, the other had blizzards and mended hockey sticks.

Stafford was the one to first tell me that Tobias never cried. I hadn't noticed it.

"No no," Stafford said, his pant legs drooping beneath his boots one afternoon, his stomach bare and his earmuffs askew, as he went about practising his wrist shot, and slipping and sliding across the small bumpy rink he had made.

"Tobias don't cry — he never cries."

"Why?"

"I don't know — " Stafford said, "You can pinch him, and punch him, and yell at him and he won't — even Jimmy J. never made him cry — when Jimmy J. took the water hose at him — and it was cold — he didn't even cry. "

"Why not?"

"I don't know," Stafford said, looking at me in a mystified way. Stafford also said he had tried to get him to cry, but couldn't manage it. He had sat on the bed and had pulled his ears. He had pulled his right ear until he hauled Tobias' head sideways and then he had gone around and pulled the left ear.

"He must be some tough if he don't cry," I said, spitting to show how tough I was.

I remembered Michael in the great fight with the boy from Skunk Ridge, when he had his head cut open.

Cold, anger, fear, hunger, and neither of them cried.

Years later I was at a university luncheon. And a woman mentioned in passing conversation about a child, living in foster homes, and adopted by her when he was eight years old, who would never cry — because he had learned by the time he was three that crying never solved anything for him.

One night she went into his bedroom and saw him, sound asleep, tears running down his cheeks.

I was asked in Spain about the mythology of my sport by the woman who got us our stick. What attracted me to it? Wasn't it a violent sport? I answered her this way: That it was more like soccer than baseball. And she seemed to accept this.

I suppose it is hard to give hockey a mythology the way people do with baseball. The great game — a full count with two out and the bases loaded in the bottom of the ninth. The echoes fall flat on the metal scrapers and shovels that litter our dooryards, the ice that pans and riddles our streets. The wind and snow over windows covered in plastic and the smell of wood smoke on bright frozen evenings down on the river.

Our great games are so *fast* there is no *singular* moment of reflection. Yet Lemieux takes a pass from Gretzky and buries a wrist shot to beat the Soviets. There is a secret in its heart that baseball cannot know.

I told my Spanish friend that our game was no longer ours, and was being changed, slowly each and every year.

And I told her that you cannot change the game continually to suit the fans — who are not fans. You cannot dress it up to suit people south of the border. To take one degree centigrade of temperature away from those snowy nights to make people who don't *like* snow, enjoy the game, is to lie about why it is important to you, in some profound and fundamental way.

And with my country disappearing, hockey seems to be the only thing, plaything that it is, that binds us together. Bright yellow pucks and four fifteen-minute quarters is what is being discussed in those boardrooms south of us. All of a sudden you have the feeling that our Northern boys are like ancient gladiators brought in for a spectacle. They keep changing the rules to try to draw the best crowd.

Seven thousand fans turn out for a game at the Meadowlands. Yet it is, and Hamilton is not, considered a hockey market. The Winnipeg Jets are going to Phoenix, Arizona. The Quebec Nordiques — become some kind of avalanche. The names will get cuter as time goes on. Edmonton will go within a year or so. Perhaps Calgary.

The Fox network lost money showing the NHL playoffs. So you can imagine what kind of state Mr. Bettman is in. The design of the net might change — to make it look more like a basketball net — or the centre line might go again, as the old Colonel wanted. And then slowly, perhaps maybe, the ice itself will go. Rollerblades will take over. Hoola girls will dance. Or maybe disco music will play during the game itself.

Yet after all of this, the kids in my old home town will still be paying their dues out on the roads, and on the river. And we will see a heritage commercial on a movie screen to remind us that it once was ours.

I will tell you where we were going that afternoon in 1989 when Paul told me about his uncle. We were going to visit his brother Stafford who had not been home in months. Stafford did not need to be hoodwinked into believing he was going to be okay.

By 1989 everything to Stafford was a shadow. He still

managed to read with a magnifying glass. That afternoon he was reading about chess. He was going to become a great chess player — the Bobby Fischer of Newcastle.

The room he lived in was piled with books. His tiny little body was sitting in a housecoat over near the window. His beard was blond and scraggly, and behind this beard was still the same childlike smile. He had a miniature chessboard set up and was playing himself. He said he was winning but that part of him was cheating because he knew what it was he was going to do.

He knew me instantly because of my walk. On his wall was an autographed picture of Bobby Orr scoring that leaping goal against St. Louis. And of course, there was a picture of Gordie Howe.

There was a picture of kids on the rink taken in 1961. I was not in the picture, but far in the background a blurred figure stood alone. It was Michael. He looked so tiny to me now. I was at an age where he could have been my son. And in a petrified way, in my mind, whenever I thought of him, he would remain that way, a still-life in a blurred winter picture, forever. At times I would wish he had been my son, to take some of the pain away.

"That's when Michael was getting the big game going against the Bantam As," Stafford reminded me.

I had forgotten all about that. The years drifted back. In the picture there were houses that are no longer, that have been swept away. Tobias with his crinkly hair and smile. Little

Ginette with her black woollen pants and a pair of huge woollen mittens hanging onto a goalie's broom. Michael in the background. One of the nets Michael had made, which seemed so wonderfully professional to us back then, and the endless stretches of grey desolate windswept river and snow.

"Pile it on Miramichi," Stafford said, glancing over blindly at that picture and lighting a cigarette.

There was also a broomball trophy near that picture. It came from that broomball league he had joined. Everyone who ever played in the broomball league got a trophy.

There was a picture of a girl who Stafford had dated for a year or so back in the early seventies, about the time of the Summit Series when Stafford became a hippie. She had gone from his life, drifted away.

There was also his archery set. Stafford had decided to become a great archer a few years before. Often he would stand in the field behind his house, shooting arrows blindly about. Missing the target the arrows would fly into a sundeck where his neighbours were barbecuing. Finally Paul talked him into giving it up, unless he had someone to supervise him.

Stafford's day consisted of books, very few people in this rooming house, would know about: Tolstoy, Carlyle, Chekhov, Yeats. And cigarettes. And rum. He would trudge to the library for his books, and on the way back he would stop in at the liquor store, then make his way back through town to his room.

His brother's prolonged lecture to him that afternoon —

a fatherly lecture, filled with a good deal of ribald joking, didn't seem to matter. After the lecture was over Stafford offered us all a drink.

The grey afternoon filled the room. A few little house plants sat on a crooked table, along with his friend, Speedball, a little red-eared turtle.

He asked about the books I wrote and if I was ever going to do a book on him. I told him that if I did I would promise not to tell the truth.

He asked me one favour, to help expose — or do an exposé on — how magazines and newspapers in the States didn't, and couldn't, tell the truth about our sport, or what it meant to *our* hearts. Because their whole moral problem was based on hiding Canada, and its contribution.

He started to riffle through tons of papers that he had collected, clippings from the Associated Press, *Knight Ryder*, Reuter and *Sports Illustrated*. Articles any Canadian would know dismissed us. He had articles underlined and circles drawn about paragraphs. The words *liar liar pants on fire* written in some margins.

But then he took the heart out of his own request by adding, "What does it matter — I don't think anything can ever be done about it now."

And he smiled at us again, raised the glass to his lips and blinked.

On the way home Paul told me that Stafford had become a referee at broomball matches.

"A referee?" I said.

"We couldn't talk him out of it. He became a referee."

Paul was silent a second, and then he asked me if I remembered that game — the game so long ago against Boston when our home town referee, Tuff, went insane with power.

"Yes vaguely," I said.

"Stafford became mad with power. He'd blow the whistle on a breakaway, give penalties to people who'd just stepped on the floor —"

"That's too bad," I said.

"'Are you blind?' they'd yell at him. 'Who told you —' Stafford would yell back. My dad and my brother would go to the rec centre to protect him. One night a few of them beat him with their brooms — as he tried to crawl to the door. 'I'm the ref,' he kept saying. 'It's my job — it's what I do.'"

Stafford finally retired from refereeing. But he still was in a hockey pool, with three town councillors, and the mayor, and had made himself captain of his team. He would trade players without his partner's knowledge. Last year when they thought they had won the pool, he had to inform them that he had traded three-quarters of their players away, "on spur-of-the-moment deals" and they had lost seven hundred and sixty dollars.

"That's too bad," I said.

He had gotten in a fight in the town hall with a councillor over this.

"That's too bad," I said.

He was now going to start his own hockey pool — and make it nationwide. He would be at the centre of a vast wheel of hockey pools and would run them by computer from his room. Although he didn't have the slightest idea about computers yet he was sure it would work.

"You know what the trouble was with *his hockey pool* don't you?" Paul said, as we walked along a part of the King George Highway, where we could see our vast and sweeping river.

"What was the trouble?"

"Well of course it was this: He will have nothing to do with a Swede, or a Russian — he had one Czech player once, but got rid of him for Pat Flatly. Finally, he works his pool around so he will have nothing but Detroit Red Wings — with Mark or Marty Howe."

"That's too bad."

"Now no one wants him in a pool — and so he has taken up chess."

"Is he good at chess?"

"Not very. He has to continually cheat against himself to win."

FOURTEEN

THE BANTAM AS MADE IT to the finals in our North Shore in 1961. They were to do better as time went on. They beat Campbellton by a goal, and just missed making it to the provincial championships. For the next five or six years we *who could never ever do it* would follow those players about the Maritimes. They would bring us some of the best high-school hockey — along with our arch-rival Chatham — that the river has ever seen. A few, as I said, would get a chance at the pros. A few like Phillip Luff, as I said, would struggle for years to attain what was impossible for them.

I remembered this as people remember things, by association. Paul was talking to me that afternoon in 1989 about Stafford and his chess, his hockey pool and of his request to me that I write something about hockey, and how it pertains to us.

I suddenly thought of the dance. The dance that was given for the benefit of the Bantam As after their season, just before we went on our trip to Boston.

It was held in the church basement, and everyone went

to it. The Midgets and Juveniles and Bantams danced. There were records playing. Elvis and Fats Domino, Buddy Holly.

There were also records of Frank Sinatra and Hank Williams. Strange jiving dances we've mostly forgotten now.

"Little Darling" played all afternoon.

Kids like myself spent the afternoon and early evening — the dance got over at 8:30 — running about drinking Coke and eating cookies that were donated by the mothers.

Some of the older boys had girlfriends but most of us didn't know what a girl was. The windows were blank, and the cold afternoon seemed to seep through. Most of the girls danced by themselves, their faces red, their hands sweaty, their dresses twirling about. They actually wore bobby socks.

And in the midst of this memory, a moment. Stafford, dressed in a white shirt and tie, his blue blazer buttoned, his brown shoes polished to a shine, dancing next to a crowd of girls jiving together.

He did everything they did — except he did it by himself.

And then he did other things too — crawled about on the ground, with his hands up in the air, showing them the bottom of his feet, and then trying to stand up like a cossack. He kept bumping into them and saying, "Excuse me." And he kept trying to wave me over to dance with him, but I wouldn't.

"Get out of here, squirt," one of the girls finally said pushing him away.

"Peewee," Stafford said innocently, "De-fen-ce — Snap Dragons."

He danced in and about them as if he was stickhandling down the centre of the ice, passing the greatest players in the world, singing along to a song he knew and they didn't seem to understand.

I left for Boston the next afternoon, a house league Peewee with a group of Bantam As — in my father's Buick — heading down, past Fredericton into Maine. I lay most of the way in the space between the back seat and the back window, listening to songs, and chewing licorice.

We were giving up some of the playoffs, because we wouldn't be able to get them on American television (really nothing much has changed in that regard in 35 years). I would miss the elimination of Montreal. Although they had finished first in 1960–61, they were a tired team. Montreal was like Bonaparte's army. Over that season, though tops in the league, and Stanley Cup champions, Les Canadiens were much like the French army after the Battle of Borodino, outside of Moscow. Though they seemed victorious, they were mortally wounded, not only physically, but morally.

The one thing very interesting about the trip down to Boston was travelling with my dad. My dad has narcolepsy — the sleeping sickness — so he would often be sound asleep at various points in the trip while still behind the wheel, and still travelling at 60 miles an hour.

The others in the car wouldn't know this. Nor would we divulge this information to them. That is, that the man driving them was dead to the world. They'd all be sitting in the back seat singing hockey songs.

My brother and I *would* know. We'd continually watch for the sign; his head to drop, with his hat pushed forwards. My brother and I had lived with this so long we hardly worried about it. Every now and again we'd yell:

"Father — *run*! Father! Run run run!"

And by God that's what would happen. He would pull over on the freeway — a 210-pound man. And he would jump out of the car, and start to run away — oblivious to where he was,until he became a spot on the horizon.

"Anything wrong?"

"What's the trouble?"

"Where is your dad going?"

"Is he a criminal?"

My brother and I would be silent, as you usually are when keeping a family secret. And then the spot would grow bigger and bigger, and there he'd be, on his way back.

Dad would get back in the car, give one of his character-istic smiles, shake the sleep out of his head, put the car back into drive, and of course, pop a speed pill. (He had a pre-scription for them. He could take four of them and go to sleep. One of them would keep most men awake for thirty-two hours.)

This was a constant of our hockey trips all over the Maritimes in the winter. The kids would invariably say that the trip was nice but that my father was strange. Sometimes kids would say, "Jeez your father's funny when he's drunk."

And I would nod.

He had tried to be a fighter pilot in the Second World War.

Down in Boston, the first thing I noticed on the old brown garage door of the old house on a street in one of the vast suburbs, was what I *didn't* see. That is the brown garage door was clean. It had no ball or puck marks on it from slapshots. It had no nub marks from hockey sticks leaning against the garage. It had a basketball hoop over it, with a torn-out net.

And Boston was so large. And everywhere I went with my all-knowing uncle I was introduced as "a hockey player from Canada" and every time my uncle said this I was immediately hugged.

"God bless you – a hockey player from Canada."

Some men actually had tears in their eyes. My uncle was often filling up and wiping his face. So was Mel who was on the hockey committee for the local Rotary.

The idea seemed to be that we hockey players had made it down by some great resources known only to us – we had traversed an abyss. The team had not been invited down by the Rotary Club, we had swam – pulled out of the icy water by the American Coast Guard.

So of course we all went along with this. We were heroes – hockey players from Canada.

We went to the tallest building in Boston and looked out over the largest city I had up until that time been in. A building that had as many people in it as my home town.

And then we were taken to see an aircraft carrier.

The young American sailors showed us about, and one asked me where I was from.

"I come from New Brunswick."

"Where is New Brunswick?"

"North of Maine —"

"Hell, boy — there ain't nothin in the world north of Maine."

I told him that was not true. That the town I was in had just about almost, counting everyone up, going door to door, five thousand people.

He informed me that the carrier I was on, had about, going berth to berth, and counting everyone up — five thousand people.

"Well, see — we're even on that," I said, and coughed.

Everything was bigger than life. And I got the impression that that was why my uncle was trying to be bigger than life himself. He sat in a large chair, smoked large cigars and had my cousin run back and forth with highballs.

"Get me 'nother hah — ball," he would say.

The hot dogs were about two feet long. If you ordered a hamburger in a restaurant it came with enough meat to feed a family of four.

Of course, not only did they not know that the Stanley Cup was happening, they had heard nothing at all about the Trail Smoke Eaters winning the World Championship. I tried to pick my time to tell my uncle this. There were people from the Rotary committee, who had been invited over to his house.

And my father and I sat with them (my brother, as a player, was billeted in another home). They were all drinking highballs. My father who was almost a total teetotaller, held a highball in his hand, his head slumped to one side, as if he had gone into alcoholic shock. I've never remembered my father in any other position, except with his head slumped to the other side.

I tried to pick my shot – like Marciano did against Jersey Joe Walcott. Take your time – get beaten about – -and then, one right hand, and down he goes in a heap at your feet.

"Uncle Ralph."

He looked over at me – a smile on his face, his face flushed from highballing it all day.

"Guess what?"

"What son?"

"Do you know what happened a few weeks ago?"

"No son – what happened a few weeks ago?"

It was on the tip of my tongue – everyone had turned politely to listen to me – and I was going to tell them. When, suddenly Treasurer Mel spoke up: so both his sentence and mine came out at the same instant, colliding objects in the same moment in space and time.

"Canada won the World Championship" … *was instantly sucked into the black hole of* … *"Boys, we can't get any ice time for the games."*

Everyone turned to Mel. Even I turned to Mel. The little simplistic and saucy smile on my face had disappeared.

Mel didn't know that when he asked to rent the rink for these exhibition games against "some fine Canadian boys," that he reserved it on the day after the Ice Follies. Which meant that the ice was out of the arena. Something he, as an unwitting new member to the ice-hockey Challenge Cup hadn't a clue about, nor taken the time to find out.

"The Ice Follies are pretty well the last thing going," Mel said, in a tone that made us want to apologize for not knowing this. "I went over to the rink last night — the ice has been taken out — " His tone suggested that since he was new to the Challenge Cup he would blame *us* for not informing him about this. He had a brief laugh and finished his drink.

We all sat there stupefied. I was numb from the toes up, and the ears down.

"Hells bells — phone around and try to get another rink," my uncle said, high on highballs.

Mel went to the phone. Though it was March, a false spring day had warmed to 75°F and Mel was wearing khaki shorts and a top, showing his huge whitish biceps.

In an hour he came back.

We all were silent. He had a slip of paper, with names and dates, and times on it. He looked nervous and agitated. The idea of hosting something had taken a peculiar turn.

There was a rink in Connecticut he said, looking at the paper, but the Canadian boys would have to cough up some money for air travel. Connecticut was certainly a long way away — to have a game of hockey.

"There is a place in Maine — they told me to phone — but I thought I'd come back and ask you guys first."

Everyone was silent. A desperate nervous silence entered the room and held us there.

Mel said it wasn't his fault. And I looked at this man, who just yesterday was kissing me and hugging me and slobbering all over me as a Canadian hockey player. Now, his eyes glassy, he looked something like a natural born killer.

Mel started to take offence at something. He spoke about being treasurer of the Rotary, and how everything was left on his shoulders. That everything was going to be blamed on him. Then he laughed, looked acutely at me.

"So you're a hockey player," he said. Still looking at me, with his brooding eyes, he said he felt certain that hockey was now out of the question. He dared me to deny.

"Well I planned to have a game," I said.

"Plans change," Mel said. I stared at my father.

My father asked if there was another rink within a radius of 40 or 50 miles. That was all he was prepared to travel.

Already the news had spread and the phone was ringing.

The air, the drinks, the clinking of glasses, my uncle's white sock feet became excruciating. The whole dimension of the trip had changed.

Mel then began to calculate money, air travel, bus tickets and then of course a three-hundred-dollar rental fee for the rink. He looked more and more and more exasperated, and he kept trying half-heartedly to convince us that this could happen to anyone. Then he said there was a very good chance — an 80 per cent chance — to have a basketball game.

"You like basketball, son?" he said.

By this time I was nervous. Even my uncle was nervous. Mel looked at me.

"You like basketball?" he said again.

I could hear the ice clink in his highball glass.

"Basketball is just about as fine a sport as there is," Mel said.

We all then began to agree that this wasn't Mel's fault. The more we said this, and the more highballs Mel drank, the more he wanted people to apologize to him.

They gave us our friendship Challenge Trophy, that they had won from us in Newcastle, back. But it wasn't the same. Losing the Canada Cup for the only time in 1981 to the Soviets, and not allowing them to take the Cup out of our country, reminded me of that day in 1961 — and how disheartened I was. I was disheartened on that occasion in 1981 also, for exactly the opposite reasoning I suppose.

We had a game of basketball. The boys tried their damndest, and played their guts out. Phillip Luff got fouled and broke a finger.

Mel was frantically cheering his boys on. He didn't want to give any quarter. It wouldn't have mattered if they had.

The final score was 87–19.

I told my uncle that we had invented the game. He said he knew.

FIFTEEN

THEIR UNIFORMS LOOK RATHER strange, kind of psychedelic. Like a jagged maple leaf or a crack of lightning cutting the sky in two.

We forget how wonderful some of the *other* players played. Brad Park, Rateille, Gilbert, Bill White, Ellis, Stapleton. Some of us back then may have wondered why Henderson was on the team. It is strange to think this now.

It is strange to think also of how cocky I was when the series started. How after the boos in Vancouver by our own fans during the fourth game, I felt ill.

Esposito, who spoke to us that night after the loss in Vancouver did as much as anyone to win the series for us. Oh, there were others all right and he could not have ever done it alone. But *he* was the one who rose to the occasion and who never gave in.

This is the one comment Tretiak made about Team Canada back in 1972. That the one great lesson the Russians learned from the series is that Team Canada would not give up.

They did everything to try and make us give up. Phone calls in the middle of the night to our players, and kids all over the ice when we went to practise. They wanted us to give up — psychologically — emotionally.

We couldn't, you see. Not then. It was more than just a game to us. We existed with it, and if it was forgotten then we could not exist without it. Without hockey the country would not *exist*. Not in the way it *should*. We would not have been able to win without French Canadian boys like Cournoyer or Savard. Or English boys like Clarke or White or Henderson.

That was the secret.

We were, on those September afternoons years ago, playing thousands of miles from home in a hostile arena with hostile fans and officials, with all the dignitaries of the Russian Politburo watching, and with many of our intellectuals scoffing, proving in both French and English, our country to each other.

This is what the great Russian players — and they were great, Kharlamov, Yakushev, Petrov, Shadrin — make no mistake — they were the greatest players the Canadians had ever faced with the greatest goalie — this is what they didn't see, and did not understand.

Perhaps we did not understand it quite as well back then either. Perhaps we lost it again over the years.

Cournoyer passing to Henderson was proving Canada to themselves.

If you think that you are a Canadian then my boy I will show you I am a Canadian too — if they check me from behind I will get up, if they kick and slash I will get up. If we play three against five for fifteen minutes I will get up. I too am a Canadian. They will not take this away from me. Nor, can I see, will they ever take it away from you. At the moment they think we are defeated we will have just begun. I will prove forever my years on the river on the back rinks, on the buses, on the farm teams. I will prove forever that this is what has shaped me. No one will then ever take this away. This is our country. This is our country!

The Russians scored two goals within a minute to defeat us in the fifth game — to put us behind 1—3—1 in the tournament. At home it may as well have been September of 1939. We had to win the last three games on Soviet ice, to win the series. My uncle was in town from Boston that month, and he looked at me, I believe with a good amount of sadness.

He had to leave soon after the fifth game, and the games weren't shown in United States. It was *their* NHL — *their* greatest players. But what did it matter to them?

"We will win," I said, shaking his hand at the driveway.

"Why do you think you will win?" he asked. He must have thought I was crazy.

"Because we *have* to," I said. And I turned and walked back to the house.

Most people (except some of the Canadians themselves) had given up on us.

My uncle worked in Canada off and on. He could speak French and so his area was Quebec and the Maritimes. He was older now, haggard. The years had not been so good to him. His son had been killed in Vietnam; the cousin of mine. This was part of the reason for his sad disbelief in my certainty that we had to win. After the fifth game we were behind 1–3–1, with three games left. All of these games to be played in Moscow, where the quota of penalties was in the ratio of 4 to 1 against us.

There was no reason for such certainty in *his* life anymore, and there never had been before in *mine*. So he was bemused by this. I thought, looking at him, of that night long ago in Boston. I wondered what had happened to Mel, to the old arena where the Ice Follies had taken place. I remembered his son playing with his team. How he had looked over at me once and smiled.

My uncle shook my hand and wished me luck. I turned and walked back to the house.

It was the last time I was to see him.

I travelled back and forth from Fredericton to Newcastle during that Summit Series. And I saw both sides of my country's reaction.

It was not that Fredericton was so different in its level of patriotism, it was that I knew very few Canadians in Fredericton in 1972 — and those few I did know were not great sports fans. Some did not even know a series was going on. The others I knew were sure that if we lost it would be a great lesson *taught us*. They did not understand that there was no lesson in this except the ones that we had to teach ourselves.

But my problems were minimal compared to Stafford Foley's. After the fourth game, the one we lost in Vancouver, I got a phone call. It was a low, tiny voice, born out of fear. "Hi Davy — who you think's going to win?"

"Who is this?"

(long pause)

"Taff."

"Stafford?"

"Yes."

"Canada."

"I suppose you've seen all the games so far?"

"Yes I have — why? Have you missed any?"

"Them all — ya."

"You *missed* them all?"

"Ya — I'm into different things now — you know."

"No — I don't know — what do you mean different things?"

There was another longer pause. There was static on the line. "Melanie — you know Melanie — we've moved in together, you know so I don't watch it."

Stafford had fallen head over heels in love. The woman did not love him. But Stafford didn't see this side of things. He only knew that he himself was in love.

The Summit Series occurred in the midst of the flow of radicalism in the universities. It was a strange phenomenon that gave the series a peculiarity, of left–right, competitive-non-competitive polarization. That this was a part of the nation at this time might not seem important when speaking of hockey. But it was important, because you could gauge the absolute grain of a person in how they reacted to Canada's initial losses, and final victory.

In the seventies during the back-to-the-land movement we, living in the rural communities, were the ones who witnessed this phenomenon first-hand. Many of the people coming from the cities of Toronto or Chicago or Montreal brought with them all the attitudes of their cities. It was a very strange phenomenon — one that was borne out of and relied upon a kind of cynical naivety about the world.

Stafford was in love with a woman who had come from Newcastle but who had adopted everything that was trendy about the world. She was a vegetarian, and a non-violent human being. It was to this regimen that Stafford had now strait-jacketed himself. He was wiggling about, and banging his head against the padded cell during the greatest series that would ever take place.

Stafford did her laundry — two pillowcases full at a time. He would make sure he separated the whites from the colours, and use non-static sheets in the dryer. Then he would fold all of her clothes in neat little piles, whistling as he did.

But I had the feeling that for her Stafford was some kind of intellectual investment, some strange little experiment. The way he reacted at that time to her was like a child continually being sent out on an egg hunt — and never quite finding the egg.

She moved to live in a farmhouse with a group — there were other farmhouses with other groups. And Stafford went with her in the hot summer of 1972 — which of course was not as hot as the summer of 1975.

They worked the land — or said they worked the land. I saw a chicken once, four pigs. There was a horse and, as far as I can tell, a goat.

This was as much a part of Stafford's life as anything so I mention it now. He tried to do all the right things. He had brought Melanie home to meet his family — asked her to go on dates. All of which she didn't respond to. Over that desperate spring of 1972 he had had a huge flower painted on the trunk of his father's car — he didn't drive himself, but had his father drive him about. A huge daisy with a peace sign. Stafford and Melanie sitting in the back seat.

He began to talk to his parents about the inevitability of class warfare — and his personal struggle against the establishment which his parents belonged to.

They would sit in their modest living room while Stafford would elaborate on his destiny to reshape the political and economic landscapes of Canada.

"Yes — I can see that — I can understand —" Mrs. Foley would say, looking nervously at her husband.

This was the problem, over that dry September, with the game of hockey. It was pro-establishment.

He couldn't believe that Melanie did not want him to watch it. This is true. It is also why I took her attachment to him as a kind of experiment for her.

Stafford had left everything behind to live with his girl. But he was not the leader of the group. A man named Malcolm was head of the group. Malcolm was older, and said he was a draft-dodger — although I never fully believed that he was. He strummed a guitar and sang Woody Guthrie. And he decided, in their group, what was to be said and not said, done and not done. (That this kind of virulent authoritarian strain was in the back-to-the-land movement does not bode well for even the simplest of human endeavours.)

"Staff," I said kindly, "this is the life-and-death struggle of Canadian hockey — you *have* to watch it. You have to be a part of it. It's *no good* without you."

"Listen," Stafford said, after the fourth game, "their backboards are funny, and their ice is large — besides it's their referees from now on — I don't know. You have to watch them — they'll be able to move much freer down along the wings — but of course so will we — so will we."

He sounded like an old soldier sadly giving advice, even though he'd been ordered to stay out of the action.

When the Russians scored off those funny backboards — twice that I saw, but especially Shadrin's goal in the eighth game — I remembered Stafford's advice.

I believe that the '72 hockey series, as great and as nation-building as it was, broke up more than one relationship in this country of ours. It polarized people. Friends of mine, a few of them well-known Canadians, I have never had the same respect for.

Stafford was an emotional wreck. He knew when every game started and ended. He almost knew by osmosis who had won.

Melanie would send him on errands all over the property. Tell him to go down to the brook for water, or into the shed and slop the pig.

"Someone has to go out and muck out the barn," Malcolm would say, and he would look about the kitchen, his eyes resting on all their childlike faces. "And someone has to come with me in to town, get the groceries and stop off at the Black Horse for a draft." Malcolm would take a drink of tea and honey, and clear his throat. "Stafford — you go and muck out the stall — Melanie — you come with me into town."

Hockey was imperialism run riot for Malcolm, who came from the mid-western United States, and had belonged at one time to a writer's group.

So during the fifth game, Stafford had to go sit in the barn with the horse. He was allergic to horses. His eyes watered, and he could barely breathe. He would try to lead the huge workhorse about, and the horse would simply drag him all over the lawn. If he had not loved Melanie he would never have done this.

This sounds exaggerated, but it is not. As a matter of fact I have toned it down. I could not mention all the things

Stafford went through for this thin and nervous young woman who always dropped acid when she and Malcolm went out to watch the fireflies, because you certainly would not believe me.

As Yeats has said, poor Stafford only managed "to flatter beauty's ignorant ear."

It didn't matter to her then. I remembered this all when I saw her picture in his little room in 1989, the day he was having the chess game against himself. Perhaps in later years, somewhere — on some rainy sidewalk in some city — she looked at her reflection and remembered him also.

This happened right at the moment of a Super Series. It happened in the dazzling brilliance of some of the greatest hockey games that were ever played. It happened when the only player on Team Canada to wear a helmet was number 19.

During the entire fifth game Stafford stayed in the barn and watched his pocket watch. He would think about how the line changes were going, who was on the ice at that moment. He said terrible things to the horse, abusive things. He called the horse Vic Hadfield.

Stafford's naivety was enhanced by bravery. One would never have worked so well without the other. I supposed he embodied the best our nation has to offer in this regard. And it was during the sixth game where his naivety gave way, and his bravery took over.

He decided to leave Melanie for a hockey game.

She accused him of not understanding her, or caring about her finer feelings — that unlike himself, she and Malcolm were feelinged individuals. This crisis in Stafford's life was just a blip on the radar screen back then.

It had nothing very much to do with me, for I had lost track of Stafford at that time, as I had lost track of so many.

The Russians were brilliant. If they were not so, it would not have been a Summit Series. If they were not so, there never would have been any argument over who was better.

Some of the greatest players I have ever seen have been Russian — Yakushev, Kharlamov, Maltsev, Shadrin, Petrov — from the '72 series. The list is substantial. But let me tell you something. We threw a team together in three or four weeks as always — in between our regular season as always. The Russians practised for a year, as always, to get ready for this.

My friends, we were, and are better. We *were* and we *are* better, as long as we wish to be. The Soviets had two hundred million souls, we had twenty million.

Nor did we just do this on our *will* though our players embodied our country's *will* at that time. Nor did we just do it on our *guts* though our players exhibited plenty of that.

We had finesse, balance and brilliance to match anything the Russians, or the Russian referees did. Yakushev was absolutely great in front of the net, Esposito was better. Our defence playing, often two men short, was nothing less than spectacular.

So in this way I am answering what Stafford asked me years ago to answer. I am answering the *Sports Illustrated* article on Team Canada of 1987. I am answering the *Miracle on Ice* movie of 1981. I am answering the *Knight Ryder* article on Fetisov printed in our sports section of the paper in September of 1995.

I am answering it for Canadians in a country that doesn't even seem to exist anymore.

I am answering the article that said hockey was born on the lakes and rivers to the North, in Canada, and perfected in the far off Soviet Union. And Fetisov was the greatest defenceman who ever lived. That my friends is a lie. It is a lie born out of misinformation and unobservance. It is a lie manufactured for the times we live in. Orr was far greater.

On any given day, I would put my money on Coffey. The rest is simply blather.

I am answering these things for Ginette and Tobias and Michael. During the '72 series we began to get to know the Russians. And we gave them credit for doing things we supposedly did not know how to do. Like pass and stickhandle. But it is useless to measure these things, because I do not want to nor should I take anything away from the greatness of the Soviet players. Certain people will always make more excuses about why we won that series, than they would have if we lost. But I will tell you — we were and are better, then and now. It is everyone's game — yet it is *ours*.

If that's nationalism in sport, don't ever forgive me.

SIXTEEN

I CAME BACK HOME, from Boston, in early April of 1961. I would not see Boston again until I went down to a conference on writing in 1989.

It was snowing when we got home and let the other boys off at their houses. Big, droopy, wet flakes fell over our dark little streets. My father had made it back — which was always a celebratory affair for us.

Because of my name (not anglicized but actually English) I had sometimes considered myself a long distant cousin of Rocket and Henri Richard — and told people that perhaps in the fourteenth or fifteenth century we had the same mother or father.

But Montreal and Toronto were gone from these playoffs. It would be a Detroit and Blackhawks final. It was an *American* final. There was a picture of the Golden Jet in our paper the morning of the first game. He looked a bit like Tab Hunter.

I did not know who to go for. It didn't matter much to

me, nor to most of us who were either Toronto or Montreal fans. But it mattered to Stafford.

It was a Detroit final and Stafford was back wearing his shoulder pads and Detroit sweater to school. He was, of course, insufferable. He would look over at me, his nose in the air and say, "Montreal? Was it Montreal you were cheering for — Les Habitants?" He would shake his head at my lack of insight.

"It takes time to build a real team," he would say to me on the way home, "You can't expect Montreal to be good overnight."

In reality in Canada, there are two kinds of hockey fans — Montreal fans, and everyone else. The Montreal fan is, by and large, gracious, kind and magnanimous in victory. There is no real dispute about this. The other fan, *everyone else*, is a peculiar kind of individual — vindictive, mean and spiteful. They are generally vindictive, mean and spiteful against the Montreal fans, who they envy continually, who they see in a kind of glowing light, who they cannot approach without trepidation. Yet the Montreal fans have no need, no *desire* to really be worshipped. They have never demanded this.

This is what Stafford was going through with me. It was payback time, and he could not help but gloat. He wondered why no-one could see Montreal's failure coming.

Whenever Montreal lost it was as if a plague had been put upon my house. It was as if I had boils, or locusts. The whole house seemed doomed. That April my youngest brother had an entire snout full of chicken pox, and wore black mittens taped to his wrists so he wouldn't scratch himself silly. He lay in his crib looking up at us, chicken pox sticking out of his hair and his ears, and in his throat, patting at his cheeks with his big mittens and crying, "Mitt — ttreeealllll." *Or so it seemed*.

My father almost always dressed in a blackish kind of suit. My sister wore a dark blue convent uniform, and a Inquisitorial cross as she walked silently about the house, passing in the hallway without speaking.

We sat in the dark — of course, this will *seem* exaggerated to *some* — but this was Stafford's hour. Stafford's moment to shine. And he did such an exacerbating job of it that he made enemies everywhere. He was like the grasshopper who teased the little industrious ant in summer. He did not know that the wind would ever blow again.

Who took advantage of this? Well I didn't because I was too stupid. I became his only friend. (Because once I did, he stopped teasing me about Montreal. I became a hysterical Detroit fan as long as the playoffs were on.) Even his brothers turned against him. They were all going for Detroit when the series started and all cheering Chicago by the end.

But it was not his twin brother Darren, his older brother Paul, his younger brothers Greg or Simon. It was not Michael, or Tobias, or myself who got him rattled. It was not even poor Ginette who still waited for us outside on the street because she was scared to come to the door. It was Garth who rattled him to his bones. Garth, the boy who carried his books like a girl and believed in Santa Claus until he was fifteen.

Garth did not know hockey but he knew business. He had an instinct for an accident waiting to happen. In his later life he would earn hundreds of thousands of dollars because of this, selling fish and chips, and take big trips to Florida. The accident waiting to happen was Stafford. Stafford did not know he was an accident waiting to happen. He was too sure of himself. He bet his money, he bet his shoulder pads, he bet his Detroit sweater — he finally bet his skates.

Garth had no passion for hockey at all. He knew nothing about hockey — that was what made it so entirely infuriating. He could pretend he did. Hockey fans seem to invite these neophytes into their camp. The neophytes are incorrigible at going along for the ride — being one with popular opinion. They never take a chance, but it is the very pedestrianness of their natures that makes them out to be winners. They have only the passion of the moment and the passion of the group. They will always be in the inner circle, because they are loath to stand on their own. They will never be great fans but they will be *accurate* fans. They will love Bobby Orr without knowing a thing about Boston. They will make money off of the Russians. They will bet on Sweden and Forsburg, against Canada and Cory Hirsh, without batting an eye, and think that all your torment and love of country is deliciously funny, because they are *proper* when it comes to the game.

This is exactly what was played out that faraway April of 1961, between Stafford and Garth. Neither of them knew that they represented the two branches of hockey, that they would evolve through Stafford into one kind of fan and through Garth into another quite different kind. That Stafford's branch would not be able to bend with the times. That Garth's branch would be sickeningly accommodating to the moment. Stafford's branch would invite disdain by both the intellectual and business, and it would die off when the country was no more. Garth's branch would invent slogans like: "It's good for the game."

Garth was very jolly this whole time. He took an actual cynical delight in torturing Stafford. After the first game he had Stafford's pet snake. Worse for Stafford, Sawchuk was hurt. This was a diversionary problem for the entire series that played favourably into Garth's hands, unknown to Garth himself, who never watched a game. He was always in bed at eight o'clock.

Stafford's big thing was to win the Stanley Cup, and like an obsessed gambler or, for a more proper correlation, like Hitler's operation Barbarosa against Russia in 1941, he poured everything he could into it.

Hockey took a great upturn on the road too, after a few weeks of sabbatical, and on the river, which still had its ice. There were games now after school every evening. Now we were Sawchuk, or Hank Bassen, or Glen Hall or Stan Mikita, Delvecchio or Howe.

Though the nights were brightening up, the air was still cold and sharp; the wind from the river could still cut through you. And Michael, who had never gotten to play for the Bantam All-Star team, was planning a big game on his rink against those in our neighbourhood who had made it to those

All-Stars — and who had gone on that trip to Boston — a city Michael would never see.

It looked as if he had bitten off more than he could chew as well. For with Paul, Darren and my brother on one team, along with Ginette in the net, and Stafford, myself and Michael, with Tobias in the net, on the other, it didn't look like much of a contest was going to happen.

But this was *the* game that was going to be played — and like all games that are played with makeup teams, it happened by accident. It happened over an argument between Paul and Michael about who between them had the hardest slapshot. I thought they were both about equal.

But Michael envied Paul. Paul was growing larger and stronger by the day — Paul's life had so much potential. He was a Foley whose father owned a tire garage. Perhaps this was what underlined the quest for the rink and the game. Perhaps Michael realized that his life was doomed, and in this doom — he wanted to make a stand. Make a stand with nothing against everything.

He would throw himself at *them* headlong, and he would pick *us* as his partners. Partners who did not know how tragic his stand was, but who also knew instinctively the losing odds.

That was the secret Michael *saw* in us. And this was the game he had planned. His battle involved forgetting who he was. Involved being a water boy for men who worked the boats, involved keeping a picture of his mother in a box, involved taking care of Tobias and knowing he could not take care of him anymore. Involved buying boots for Tobias and wearing shoes most of the winter.

It was his battle.

Stafford said later that it was Hank Bassen, the backup goalie for Detroit that cost him everything. Cost him his hockey sweater and his pet snake. Because he worried about Hank Bassen. It was as if his great hockey mind seemed to make a series of blunders in 1961 that would never happen to him again. As if he was like Napoleon with a cold, Hannibal who, after Cannae, could not take Rome.

But the worst thing for Stafford was that in his jubilation, in his tirades against Chicago, and his side attacks against Montreal, he was both his only general and his enemy's only mole. That is, Stafford would talk and Garth would listen. Before this series started Garth, I am convinced, had never heard of Pierre Pilote or Stan Mikita. Nor had he heard of Glen Hall, Hank Bassen, Ken Wharram or perhaps not even Howe or Hull. But you see that did not matter. For the spy in Stafford's character spoon-fed Garth all of this.

"I hope the defence can help old Hank Bassen and stop Hull and Mikita and Pilote or we're in trouble."

"I bet they can't," Garth would say.

"Pilote won't score — he won't score."

"Bet your lousy shoulder pads he will," Garth would say.

Then the general in Stafford would take over. He would try to stop the leaks in his knowledge that had been given away by his spy.

"Well I don't want to talk about it anymore."

"I see."

"What do you mean — you see?"

"I just see you're frightened of Mikita and Hull and Pierre Pilote and are blaming poor Hank Bassen — a goalie of great stature probably. So really the faith in your team is bogus."

"Great stature — what does that mean?"

"Let's not talk about it," Garth would say, as disheartened at dishonesty and duplicity as, oh I don't know — maybe Jacques Parizeau himself.

This would go on, or at least a conversation much like this. Perhaps not in its language but in its intention as sophisticated as some political strategist.

And poor Stafford would be left wobbling in uncertainty.

"Damn it all — Garth is a hockey genius," he told us. "I can't get by him, he keeps coming up with the answers — I don't know how he has it figured out. I think he even predicted that Sawchuk would hurt his shoulder. The trick is — he's quiet — he never says anything — he's a sneaky, girlie, kind of guy — but *what he knows* is incredible."

A number of things worked against Stafford. One was his absolute openness with all his friends — a feeling that they would, because of friendship, share as much information with him as he did with them. Another was his ability to lie for these friends to himself, and always place them in the best possible light (similar to what he did with Jimmy J. and years later with Melanie). Third was his overall superstition. He was sure even years later that it was his bad luck, something in his nature, that caused the Red Wings to lose.

He wore the same socks throughout the entire playoffs. Twice his mother sneaked them from his bedroom at night and washed them, but he had them back on his feet the next morning, as wet as rags.

But the worst thing of all was how he was teased and tormented about the greatness of Chicago to and from school. He was all alone as they teased him. And so he bet his shoulder pads, his sweater, his skates, his bitten-up hockey puck, his snake.

He, too, like Michael, was taking on all comers, because he knew, he knew, he knew — he would lose.

Between games five and six — with the Hawks up 3–2 in games, Stafford was restless. I asked him to a movie with me the night before the sixth game and he babbled like an idiot about the referees, Chicago cheats, Garth. He hated Garth; Garth had become his nemesis. He had Garth figured out. Garth was not the hockey genius one might first think. "I asked him what he thought of Chicago and he told me he thought they were adorable. *Adorable*," Stafford said. "How can a person even say that about a hockey team?"

Stafford touched every pole on the way to the movie, and every pole on the way back. If he missed a pole he would go back and touch it. Then as we turned along King George Highway he began to worry about his socks. He sat down on the sidewalk, in the slush, took his boots and shoes off and switched his socks about. Two women passed by, and he looked up at them, as indifferently as if he was in his bedroom with Tobias.

He had to have them on the same feet for Detroit to have a sliver of a chance. And he had mixed them up, because his mother was dumb enough (his words) to wash them. This mixup in his socks is what cost Detroit the cup in 1961.

Game six was Chicago's. Bassen was in the net for Detroit because Sawchuk had played poorly in the fifth. However Chicago won by the same score the Trail Smoke Eaters won the World Championship in March: 5–1. Detroit's dream was over. As yet it still is.

Stafford kept his head under a couch cushion for almost the entire game. Now and then, when you looked over at him, you would see a giant cushion, and two half-blind eyes blinking from under it, as he stared morbidly at the TV.

Stafford was cantankerous after Detroit lost. He looked sad and feeble. Worse, Garth actually kept all the things he took. Stafford's twin brother Darren managed to get the bitten hockey puck back, because it had come from a Moncton Hawks' game, the only important game Stafford had ever been to. Darren brought it home and set it back on Stafford's desk.

Every night he got into bed, and lay upon a plastic sheet, and stared through the window across the hallway at the stars. He had forgotten much about his Lloyd Percival pamphlets, and when I tried to cheer him up by talking about Lloyd, he looked at me and shrugged.

SEVENTEEN

My father was president of the Recreation Council in 1961 and Gordie Howe was invited to give the talk at the closing banquet. My father picked him up at the train station, and mentioned to him, that though I had played hockey that year, I felt that I hadn't played quite well enough to deserve a dinner. So I was going to stay home.

Gordie said kind-heartedly that that was not right, and telephoned me and asked me to go, saying he wanted to see me there.

Of course I forgot all about Stafford. He came to the door and I was getting my white shirt and tie on, tucking myself together.

"Where are you going?" Stafford said.

"Oh — I guess I'll go along to the banquet."

"You said you weren't going — you talked me into not going —"

"Well — I wasn't planning to — but Gordie phoned me, wants to see me there — you know."

"Gordie — Gordie who?"

"Gordie Howe —"

Stafford looked at me. He looked at my mother. He looked at my brother. He looked at my mother again.

"Gordie Howe — the real Gordie Howe."

"Of course."

Stafford came close to me and whispered, "The one in my poem —"

"Same Gordie."

"What did he say?!"

"Just the usual small talk — you know what Gordie's like." I answered for some reason as if I was aggravated.

My mother was bent over fixing the cuffs of my pants and telling me to stay still, and I was wobbling back and forth in the hallway, with the most exasperatingly worldly look on my face that Stafford had ever seen.

I never noticed him leave.

Things were happening at the Foley's Tire Garage all over Easter — incidental things — small things. Jimmy J. went there every night to eat peanuts. It's a rather strange thing for men to leave the comfort of their home, and sit in an old garage and eat peanuts with the cold drafts forever through the great doors.

But at any rate he was back to being Jimmy J. He talked about having killed a polar bear. He talked about fishing. He talked about space ships. He had a cigarette behind his left ear and a cigarette behind his right. He hated communists. He believed he knew some.

When Paul or Mr. Foley came into the garage he would leave, two young boys following him out. But when the garage was left in charge of anyone else Jimmy J. would pop his head back in the door, walk nonchalantly over to the peanut machine, and put in a nickel.

Now the story was that he owed everyone money and his wife's hairdressing business was being put on the auction block because of Jimmy J.

Jimmy J. would always chew one peanut at a time. He had come back to the garage to tease Stafford about Detroit, but whenever Stafford saw him he would turn and walk in the other direction.

"All the NHL hockey games are fixed," Jimmy J. stated.

He liked to state this, because it gave him the moral higher ground, and an instant credential he never had to prove, about his value as a social critic of the game, as he popped one peanut into his mouth and chewed it rapidly, while jostling the other seventeen peanuts in his hand.

"You wouldn't see me watching a dumb hockey game — for I tell yas boys them are all fixed —"

This was Jimmy J.'s revelation. They were fixed and that's why he didn't watch them. He was, of course, an offshoot of the branch of Garth.

The branch of Garth flowered over many years into a variety of offshoots. And all of these offshoots have been discussed at least somewhat. It is the branch that allows us to boo Team Canada in Vancouver in 1972. The branch that allows us to believe that passion is only worthy of rednecks. The branch that makes us grovel to political correctness, and to conveniently pull the wool over our own eyes to changes wreaking havoc upon the sport.

Yet it is a branch, not without its truth, because as we know, no tree can bear fruit without truth.

Jimmy J. was an offshoot who would create a larger off-shoot. He flourished between the time of the original six and expansion. Jimmy J., although his shoot still exists, has evolved into the branch that comfortably asserts that all hockey is simply vulgar business and they wish nothing to do with it.

Stafford's branch — the branch which lost all of his snakes and things to Garth, stretched toward the sun in a different direction. His branch would create shoots and offshoots as well. The branch of Stafford, and the branch of Garth, would become more and more alienated from one another. The two worlds of hockey, the two solitudes.

The night of the dinner Jimmy J. left his house, that was now in darkness, and made his way down the long street toward the river, still frozen in the frozen wind, and raw temperature. He got to the garage about 8:30.

He was angry with the peanut machine. And sat there until about 9:43 talking about it. The idea that a man could spend well over an hour talking about a peanut machine may seem strange — but I've known friends of mine at the tavern who have talked for four hours straight about an axe handle. So an hour about a peanut machine and how corrupt the Foleys were to have a peanut machine like that in their garage was not so much for Jimmy J.

The other man in the garage was Mr. Comeau, the trainer, who rushed that long ago night to our goalie's aid when he hit his head on the crossbar during his warmup for the Boston game, the man who had made the statement, "It's a long way from your heart."

He was keeping the garage opened (it was Friday night) until the Foleys got back from the banquet.

Finally he gave into Jimmy J., and gave him the nickel he said he had lost in the machine the week before.

Jimmy stood up and took this nickel, with a great amount of wounded pride, and went to the machine. He put the nickel in, bent over to turn the dial.

Just then a car backfired — or so everyone thought — and Mr. Comeau fell to the floor dead with a rifle shot through the heart. He slumped and he fell, his hands still clutching some coins — and that was it. Like murder always is — it was banal.

The one other person who saw this was Paul Foley, who had just come in the door, still in his white shirt and tie.

Most people said it was not Mr. Comeau, but Jimmy J., the man was after. The man who committed the murder was found washed up on shore two months later tangled in a herring net.

— · —

For a while Paul acted normal. But soon cracks began to show. By the night of the game on the river, it was as if he was in his own world.

There were some good players on this team that night. My brother was good enough to be considered as a draft possibility in expansion. Darren was fiery and tough. Paul was a great hockey player — but that night he kept giving the puck away.

Michael — Michael was the greatest of us all.

All of our hockey sticks were broken and taped — some of them right up the handles. The nets were made of fish twine, as they were made in Nova Scotia in the 1890s. The river was as clear as a bell. Far away, up the bank, still pock-marked with dark snow the sound of a train rattled the windows of a row of dark wooden houses.

There was also a permanent smell of sulphur that meant that the air was trapped and spring was on its way. The wind would blow again out of the southeast in the next few weeks, and hockey would be over.

We played under the light of the moon, all of us wearing skates except Ginette and Tobias. We played with Stafford's bitten puck because he insisted.

The river was dark, and each of us was hit with the puck a number of times. Ginette would wobble out with her broom and take a swipe at it, and it would veer into the corner. Darren would pick it up and start up along the boards — those railway ties Michael had stolen. But someone would be there to grapple with him, or the puck or to fall upon it.

It would squirt out as Paul always said it would if you were patient. Once or twice it even wobbled to me. The idea that I was skating and holding a puck with my stick was ecstasy. Paul would come back, flip my stick up and take the puck and start back. Only to be hip-checked by Michael.

Tobias would run out in his rubber boots like a small demon, and start up the ice. He would go sprawling forward, the puck on his large goalie stick — a stick that Michael had gotten him after a Miramichi Beaver game. The puck would be lost in the middle of us.

Tobias was slashed across the wrists, and didn't make a sound. There would be an almost silent swish of a skate blade behind you and someone would be coming to ram you up against the boards or run you down.

Michael potted a goal for us and Darren had potted two or three for them. Of course we could score easily on Ginette if we could get there — that was the secret.

But they were always up near or close to our net. Tobias fought back with every tiny bit of muscle he had. And Michael and I kept coming back to help him. We were slashed on the ankles and legs, and in the light of the moon, we could see blood from where a tooth had gone through Tobias' lip.

Yet as always and quite suddenly, for Tobias and Michael, there was, because of hockey, no more *real* cold or pain, or terrified nights alone. There was no more shame. They were free.

And this is what the game was about for Ginette, Michael, Tobias, Stafford and me.

I don't think any of us had ever been free before.

We just held them that was all. It was always about our net. Once in a while Michael broke away — and he broke away like a runner out of the blocks, a horse from the gate. Suddenly he was gone with the puck, and no one could catch him, broken skates and woollen socks over a pair of torn jeans, water in his eyes.

Ginette would gallantly try to block him with the broom she had used all that year.

On her thin wobbly legs, like a young calf, and wearing a pair of black woollen slacks, a training bra under her sweater, her lovely dark hair smelling of wood smoke, she would come out to face him, bravely trying to stop what she couldn't, but once or twice actually managing to poke-check the puck away.

And back they would come.

Tobias wore no gloves. His hands were rapped more than once by Darren or my brother trying to get the puck.

His whole world became that net smelling of earth and twine that his brother had made with his own hands. They had only managed three goals. Perhaps he would have given up long before he did if he did not love Michael so much.

No matter how well, how badly we played, the game was

ours. It was what the Colonel said it was — it was in our hearts. It was life.

One place we weren't suppose to be at that time of year of course, was on the river.

Tobias had lifted the puck and it went by everyone, and drifted onto Stafford's stick. Stafford looked about, realized he was home free — that he could score the goal to tie the game. He began to skate so ferociously that he didn't move an inch.

He had a great deal of momentum however. He was laughing his head off. He was joyous. He was absolutely pleased with himself.

Then he just disappeared.

The puck trickled forth, and stopped a few inches before the net. Everything was quiet. The wind blew slightly. Michael and Paul, without thinking that they could go under also, rushed over to where he *had* been, and thrust their arms down. Took their arms out and thrust them down once more. Everything happened in slow motion — exactly as they say it does, and everyone was absolutely calm.

"Feel him?" Paul said.

"Ya I got him by the hair and the ear," Michael said.

"Haul him out."

Stafford came to the surface, spitting and howling. He was dragged to the side of the river, where the rest of us gathered around him — handing him our coats, being supportive. Telling him he'd better dry off before he went home because none of us wanted to get into trouble.

And then we all turned away from the river, away from Michael's rink, toward home.

"I could have tied the game boys — I could have scored. I could have got it. Me. Me. I could have got a *goal*," Stafford kept saying, spitting and coughing, and talking about Lloyd Percival, all the way up the hill.

He might have scored.

I never would have heard the end of it if he had.

The expansion came as they said it would. But surprisingly it did not come to Newcastle, NB. And I don't think it ever will. Although who knows?

Once in Spain years ago we watched that hockey game between Barcelona and Valencia, my wife and I, on Spanish TV. I watched the Roanoke Rebels in Roanoke Virginia, when I was down there, and followed the British ice hockey scores one time when I was in England.

I'll always be able to find or fashion a hockey stick I tell you that — even though 1961 was my last year of organized hockey, and I took up curling, as my mother prayed I would.

Those children are all gone away now. The skates the sticks have disappeared. I have not been back to my river in a long, long time, and don't think of it as my river any more. It belongs to others now. I too have gone away.

Every December when the World Junior is on, and every April when the World Championship is on, and every four years when the World Women's Championship is on it will not be hard to find me. I will be home — usually alone, in front of the television, screaming my head off. I will celebrate the women's play as much as the men, not because I am politically correct — far from it. They deserve to be celebrated. I know. I know. I played with Ginette.

Paul Foley far more than Phillip Luff could have made it to the Montreal Canadiens. He knew it. I knew it. But something happened. Perhaps it was simple fate. He walked into the garage after the banquet to tell Mr. Comeau he could go home and Mr. Comeau was ready to say something to him, which Paul was never, ever allowed to hear.

After that he concerned himself with other things. He decided one day in Grade 10 to become a missionary. And he did, and kept his humanity while doing it.

Time passed. The next year there was no rink at all on the river. In January Tobias went to live somewhere else. Michael promised him he could come back — promised him, they would stay in touch.

"Where will I go and stand — like stand there so you can come and get me?" Tobias said hopefully — tears for the first time running down his face.

After the world changed and the Beatles came I lost touch with Michael. He moved in a different circle. Became as tough as nails and could hit like a mule. He still wore his hair like James Dean, drank too much, and had a parade of sad young girls. One night coming back from somewhere there was an accident. He was thrown from a car and killed.

When their house was torn down, when I was still young enough to think I was going to become a writer, I went back to that spot, as if to examine my youth. Cattails and thorned alders grew against the pale November sky. In the tatters of the house, graced with the smell of longing and November smoke, the coat that Michael had bought Tobias with the bingo money sat crumpled up in a hole in one of the fallen walls. As if it was at one point, years before, used by someone to stop some unstoppable draft.

Stafford would never obey anyone of course. Not Paul. Not the doctors nor his poor parents who fretted and worried to death about him.

In the end he only pretended. Pretended he could watch hockey that was no more than a faint shadow on the television. Pretended he could read Yeats when he could not see the page. Pretended he could organize a hockey pool and get rid of all the Swedes, over the objections of all of those *other* more *practical* fans.

No-one wanted him in their hockey pool, calling him a man of dissension. Not a visionary, but a divisionary.

All of us suffer from the one great delusion, Paul said. We were and are all delusional spirits. The delusion is *this*. That perhaps HOCKEY — hockey can keep this country together. Hockey can save Canada — for we see to the bottom of our heart there is no Gretzky without Lemieux. Perhaps we are *that* delusional, and perhaps for one time when we really need it to — when we really want it to, a delusion can work for us instead of against us.

After a while Stafford, who had only loved Melanie, found comfort in an older woman who would come in and take care of him. He teased her unmercifully — because at times she had to bathe him. And he hid his bottles from her, and drank behind her back. She thought she was doing a very good job, and he didn't have the heart to tell her that she wasn't.

He lived in a room surrounded by his past without seeing it much anymore. Daily, he made his trips to the library and liquor store. He was gentle enough and kind enough to follow my career, because he felt it would matter to me. He tried to teach the woman about hockey — from the Stafford Foley perspective. And finally after a few weeks of instruction, he touched his breast with his hand and whispered, "It's all in here." And he smiled.

I had been out of the country (that trip to Australia), and when I got back home I packed up my truck and went into the woods for a few days, with a friend.

On the way out we stopped at a garage to telephone his wife. He spoke for a few moments and came back to the truck. He was silent for quite a while.

"It's a very warm night for November," he said finally.

"Yes."

He paused, cleared his throat, looked out the window at something. "Stafford is dead."

Stafford's lady friend had found him sitting in his chair one morning. He had died in his sleep. On his radio was that song by Leonard Cohen, the one that says there are rocket ships in the sky, and doctors but that there is no cure for love.

It kept playing, and playing like a Leonard Cohen song usually does, for a long time.

Stafford would have been proud. The next year we Canadians won back *our* World Championship after 30 bloody years of waiting.

And then *his* Detroit finally got to the finals of the Stanley Cup again. Even though they lost, they had a shot. So he certainly would have had something more to cheer about and bother everyone he knew about. And bet his shirt, and Speedball his turtle too I suppose. He was forever a man like that. He came to it honestly, like we all did.

I came back from Spain in time to see the playoffs of the shortened season — Detroit against the New Jersey Devils. New Jersey was supposed to have this wonderfully new defensive system, called "the trap."

The idea of a secret weapon in hockey is always the way to catch an audience. The idea that the game can be reduced to a foolproof system, which no mortal can get around, and which will make everyone an instant expert. The notion that we can corral the game, trap it by saying so-and-so or such-and-such is using *the trap*.

New Jersey played hockey, similar to Montreal. They won the Cup, and are now preparing to go to Nashville. Although the New Jersey coaching staff is Canadian, they have more American players than any other team — I believe. Detroit has Canadians, Americans, and Russians. In a way this made it a truly American NHL final. Stafford and I could no longer say, as we did when Chicago played Detroit in 1961, that all of the players were Canadian anyway.

During the first games of this season, the referees' emphasis on enforcing new interference rules made the game unbearable to watch. No-one seemed to know much about what they were doing. A play would just get started and the whistle would blow for some infraction, from some player trying to clear the front of his net. It reminded me of old Tuff, in our home town game against Boston.

In Saint John I took my son to an AHL Flames game. We watched as the players skated out of a smoking, air-filled dragon, and Flea Burn, the Flames mascot, did hand-stands during a light show. He did them well.

When the Flames scored the place erupted into the old familiar bedlam however.

Recently I had to attend a dinner in Toronto. As I stood in the large room, surrounded by many important people, I suddenly thought of Tobias.

A feeling of loss washed over me.

It was a strange feeling to have that moment. Men in black tie, and women in long dresses seemed to float by. I turned, and there standing three feet away was Gordie Howe.

I am not a man to impose and yet suddenly, for all our sakes — for Michael and Ginette, and for Paul and Stafford and Tobias — I was blurting out things to him. I was telling him the story about when he telephoned me, so long, long ago. I told him we all played on the rinks on the river. We too had our games. And he, Gordie Howe, smiled and acknowledged this kindly. He, Gordie Howe, spoke to me again, after 35 years, when all my past life seemed a ghost. He nodded and we shook hands.

I never betrayed Stafford. I never mentioned the poem.